SCRABBLE®
BRAND
Grams #2

Judd F. Hambrick

Harmony Books / New York

Published by Harmony Books, a division of Crown Publishers,
Inc., One Park Avenue, New York, New York 10016 and
simultaneously in Canada by General Publishing Company
Limited

HARMONY BOOKS and colophon are trademarks of Crown
Publishers, Inc.

Manufactured in the United States of America

SCRABBLE® Brand Grams are licensed by Selchow & Righter
Company, owner of the registered trademark SCRABBLE®

ISBN: 0-517-546205

10 9 8 7 6 5 4 3 2 1
First Edition

How to Play
SCRABBLE®
BRAND
Grams

Rearrange each row of letters to form a 2- to 7-letter word. Use the scoring directions to the right of each row to total your points. Seven-letter words are worth 50 bonus points. "Blanks" used as any letter have no point value. Proper nouns and foreign, slang or hyphenated words are forbidden.

There are many possible solutions. Judd Hambrick's answers can be found in the back of the book.

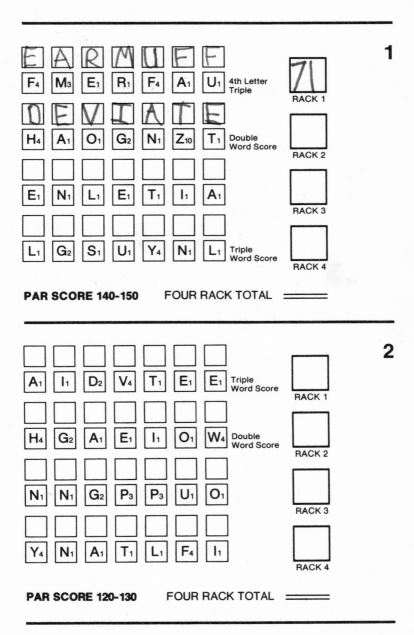

1

E	A	R	M	U	F	F
F₄	M₃	E₁	R₁	F₄	A₁	U₁

4th Letter
Triple

RACK 1

D	E	V	I	A	T	E
H₄	A₁	O₁	G₂	N₁	Z₁₀	T₁

Double
Word Score

RACK 2

E₁	N₁	L₁	E₁	T₁	I₁	A₁

RACK 3

L₁	G₂	S₁	U₁	Y₄	N₁	L₁

Triple
Word Score

RACK 4

PAR SCORE 140-150   FOUR RACK TOTAL ═══

2

A₁	I₁	D₂	V₄	T₁	E₁	E₁

Triple
Word Score

RACK 1

H₄	G₂	A₁	E₁	I₁	O₁	W₄

Double
Word Score

RACK 2

N₁	N₁	G₂	P₃	P₃	U₁	O₁

RACK 3

Y₄	N₁	A₁	T₁	L₁	F₄	I₁

RACK 4

PAR SCORE 120-130   FOUR RACK TOTAL ═══

3

K_5	D_2	H_4	D_2	O_1	A_1	C_3

N_1	T_1	C_3	R_1	I_1	E_1	A_1

L_1	R_1	U_1	P_3	O_1	E_1	S_1	Double Word Score

X_8	E_1	U_1	I_1	S_1	S_1	N_1	Triple Word Score

RACK 1

RACK 2

RACK 3

RACK 4

PAR SCORE 130-140   FOUR RACK TOTAL ═══

4

G_2	I_1	P_3	N_1	R_1	O_1	E_1	1st Letter Triple

L_1	S_1	G_2	Y_4	T_1	A_1	H_4	2nd Letter Double

K_5	E_1	M_3	L_1	T_1	I_1	R_1	Double Word Score

U_1	G_2	R_1	A_1	E_1	E_1	O_1

RACK 1

RACK 2

RACK 3

RACK 4

PAR SCORE 115-125   FOUR RACK TOTAL ═══

5

R₁	A₁	G₂	U₁	N₁	D₂	E₁	Double Word Score

RACK 1

| O₁ | D₂ | A₁ | E₁ | O₁ | F₄ | S₁ | 4th Letter Triple |

RACK 2

| A₁ | O₁ | D₂ | I₁ | R₁ | E₁ | V₄ | |

RACK 3

| P₃ | D₂ | T₁ | E₁ | O₁ | E₁ | S₁ | 4th Letter Double |

RACK 4

PAR SCORE 75–85   FOUR RACK TOTAL ═══

6

| I₁ | E₁ | blank | N₁ | T₁ | E₁ | F₄ | |

RACK 1

| G₂ | L₁ | G₂ | S₁ | N₁ | O₁ | I₁ | |

RACK 2

| R₁ | E₁ | N₁ | R₁ | E₁ | H₄ | I₁ | Triple Word Score |

RACK 3

| D₂ | R₁ | S₁ | U₁ | Y₄ | C₃ | V₄ | Triple Word Score |

RACK 4

PAR SCORE 135–145   FOUR RACK TOTAL ═══

7

Y₄	E₁	L₁	R₁	A₁	A₁	T₁

RACK 1

A₁	U₁	N₁	L₁	R₁	T₁	A₁

Double Word Score

RACK 2

X₈	N₁	L₁	R₁	Y₄	E₁	A₁

RACK 3

F₄	O₁	E₁	R₁	S₁	F₄	T₁

RACK 4

PAR SCORE 110-120   FOUR RACK TOTAL ═══

8

A₁	M₃	T₁	F₄	S₁	L₁	O₁

1st Letter Double

RACK 1

H₄	N₁	B₃	E₁	T₁	E₁	A₁

RACK 2

Y₄	A₁	A₁	S₁	A₁	T₁	R₁

Double Word Score

RACK 3

P₃	T₁	M₃	E₁	E₁	L₁	X₈

RACK 4

PAR SCORE 115-125   FOUR RACK TOTAL ═══

9

E₁	P₃	W₄	N₁	O₁	E₁	H₄

4th Letter
Triple

RACK 1

Y₄	K₅	L₁	I₁	L₁	L₁	E₁

RACK 2

C₃	S₁	J₈	T₁	E₁	U₁	I₁

Double
Word Score

RACK 3

D₂	A₁	F₄	C₃	A₁	E₁	A₁

RACK 4

PAR SCORE 90-100   **FOUR RACK TOTAL** ====

10

L₁	F₄	D₂	N₁	I₁	I₁	E₁

Triple
Word Score

RACK 1

A₁	M₃	N₁	E₁	E₁	N₁	G₂

1st Letter
Double

RACK 2

I₁	A₁	E₁	R₁	L₁	U₁	C₃

RACK 3

T₁	T₁	S₁	S₁	A₁	O₁	U₁

RACK 4

PAR SCORE 120-130   **FOUR RACK TOTAL** ====

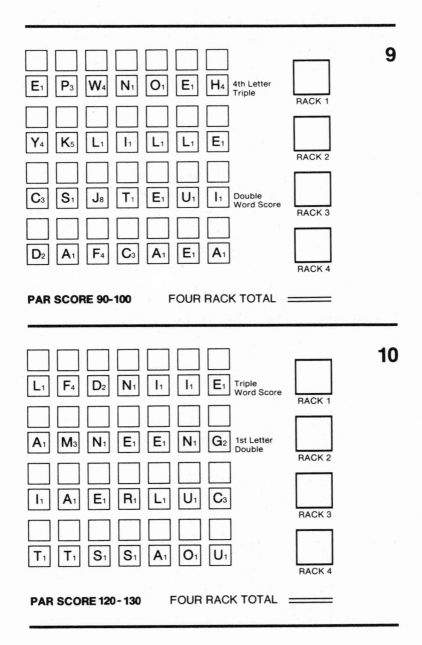

11

O₁	K₅	B₃	D₂	N₁	N₁	I₁	4th Letter Triple
R₁	M₃	N₁	E₁	A₁	E₁	G₂	
D₂	R₁	N₁	L₁	E₁	E₁	E₁	
S₁	S₁	C₃	A₁	I₁	blank	E₁	Double Word Score

RACK 1

RACK 2

RACK 3

RACK 4

PAR SCORE 150–160   FOUR RACK TOTAL ====

12

I₁	D₂	C₃	V₄	T₁	A₁	U₁	
U₁	U₁	S₁	D₂	D₂	B₃	E₁	
S₁	U₁	T₁	O₁	I₁	T₁	R₁	
H₄	T₁	P₃	B₃	E₁	R₁	O₁	

RACK 1

RACK 2

RACK 3

RACK 4

PAR SCORE 175–185   FOUR RACK TOTAL ====

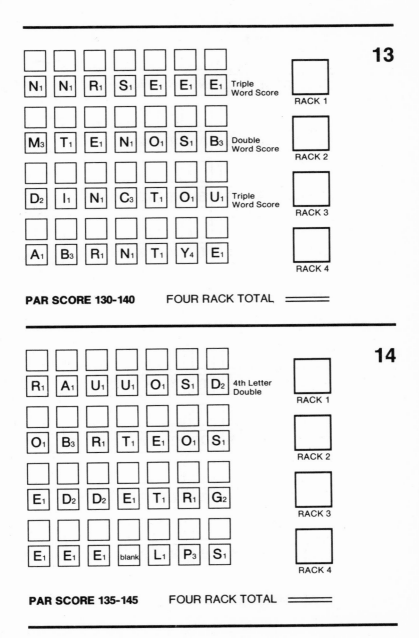

13

N₁ N₁ R₁ S₁ E₁ E₁ E₁ Triple Word Score

RACK 1

M₃ T₁ E₁ N₁ O₁ S₁ B₃ Double Word Score

RACK 2

D₂ I₁ N₁ C₃ T₁ O₁ U₁ Triple Word Score

RACK 3

A₁ B₃ R₁ N₁ T₁ Y₄ E₁

RACK 4

PAR SCORE 130-140   FOUR RACK TOTAL ═══

14

R₁ A₁ U₁ U₁ O₁ S₁ D₂ 4th Letter Double

RACK 1

O₁ B₃ R₁ T₁ E₁ O₁ S₁

RACK 2

E₁ D₂ D₂ E₁ T₁ R₁ G₂

RACK 3

E₁ E₁ E₁ blank L₁ P₃ S₁

RACK 4

PAR SCORE 135-145   FOUR RACK TOTAL ═══

15

N_1	X_8	L_1	O_1	K_5	N_1	A_1	4th Letter Triple

RACK 1

E_1	L_1	G_2	U_1	N_1	T_1	P_3

RACK 2

Y_4	U_1	A_1	O_1	S_1	T_1	P_3	3rd Letter Triple

RACK 3

N_1	E_1	C_3	I_1	O_1	T_1	R_1

RACK 4

PAR SCORE 80-90   FOUR RACK TOTAL ====

16

B_3	N_1	I_1	L_1	O_1	E_1	G_2

RACK 1

K_5	A_1	R_1	S_1	T_1	T_1	A_1	Triple Word Score

RACK 2

Y_4	L_1	C_3	E_1	T_1	U_1	R_1

RACK 3

L_1	O_1	T_1	A_1	O_1	R_1	P_3

RACK 4

PAR SCORE 95-105   FOUR RACK TOTAL ====

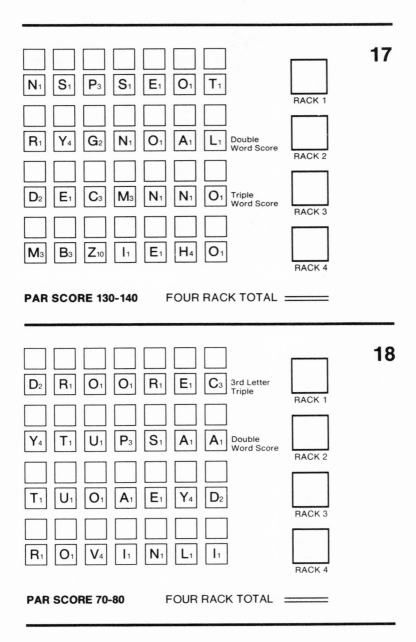

17

N₁	S₁	P₃	S₁	E₁	O₁	T₁	RACK 1
R₁	Y₄	G₂	N₁	O₁	A₁	L₁	Double Word Score / RACK 2
D₂	E₁	C₃	M₃	N₁	N₁	O₁	Triple Word Score / RACK 3
M₃	B₃	Z₁₀	I₁	E₁	H₄	O₁	RACK 4

PAR SCORE 130-140   FOUR RACK TOTAL ═════

18

D₂	R₁	O₁	O₁	R₁	E₁	C₃	3rd Letter Triple / RACK 1
Y₄	T₁	U₁	P₃	S₁	A₁	A₁	Double Word Score / RACK 2
T₁	U₁	O₁	A₁	E₁	Y₄	D₂	RACK 3
R₁	O₁	V₄	I₁	N₁	L₁	I₁	RACK 4

PAR SCORE 70-80   FOUR RACK TOTAL ═════

19

H_4	P_3	L_1	T_1	V_4	Y_4	M_3	2nd Letter Double

C_3	R_1	T_1	H_4	E_1	E_1	A_1	3rd Letter **Triple**

A_1	R_1	T_1	E_1	O_1	E_1	B_3

R_1	R_1	T_1	A_1	S_1	I_1	A_1

RACK 1
RACK 2
RACK 3
RACK 4

PAR SCORE 70-80   FOUR RACK TOTAL =====

20

A_1	Y_4	U_1	N_1	R_1	C_3	T_1	Triple Word Score

T_1	E_1	P_3	N_1	S_1	R_1	A_1

E_1	G_2	C_3	T_1	N_1	T_1	Y_4	2nd Letter **Triple**

V_4	P_3	O_1	A_1	S_1	S_1	E_1

RACK 1
RACK 2
RACK 3
RACK 4

PAR SCORE 125-135   FOUR RACK TOTAL =====

21

E_1	L_1	R_1	X_8	P_3	P_3	E_1	Double Word Score
K_5	N_1	D_2	V_4	C_3	R_1	U_1	Double Word Score
Y_4	R_1	A_1	M_3	O_1	U_1	R_1	
E_1	B_3	V_4	L_1	I_1	I_1	A_1	4th Letter Triple

RACK 1

RACK 2

RACK 3

RACK 4

PAR SCORE 95-105   FOUR RACK TOTAL ══════

22

E_1	U_1	D_2	T_1	I_1	L_1	A_1	
H_4	O_1	S_1	N_1	R_1	W_4	N_1	4th Letter Triple
O_1	I_1	M_3	P_3	D_2	Z_{10}	G_2	3rd Letter Triple
E_1	T_1	L_1	N_1	C_3	R_1	E_1	

RACK 1

RACK 2

RACK 3

RACK 4

PAR SCORE 85-95   FOUR RACK TOTAL ══════

23

T₁	G₂	M₃	A₁	E₁	O₁	N₁

P₃	Y₄	A₁	R₁	B₃	J₈	E₁

Ist Letter Triple

E₁	F₄	N₁	I₁	T₁	K₅	R₁

S₁	D₂	R₁	L₁	E₁	I₁	D₂

RACK 1

RACK 2

RACK 3

RACK 4

PAR SCORE 120–130   FOUR RACK TOTAL ═══

24

L₁	B₃	T₁	N₁	A₁	E₁	U₁

Ist Letter Triple

L₁	E₁	R₁	E₁	O₁	S₁	M₃

Double Word Score

I₁	S₁	E₁	C₃	T₁	L₁	L₁

Y₄	I₁	A₁	D₂	U₁	I₁	R₁

Triple Word Score

RACK 1

RACK 2

RACK 3

RACK 4

PAR SCORE 115–125   FOUR RACK TOTAL ═══

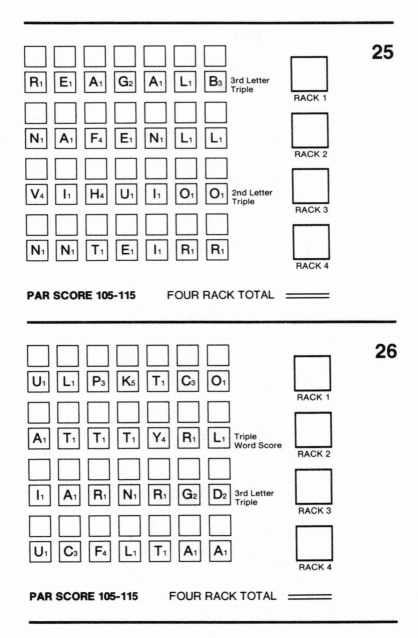

25

R₁ E₁ A₁ G₂ A₁ L₁ B₃ 3rd Letter Triple

RACK 1

N₁ A₁ F₄ E₁ N₁ L₁ L₁

RACK 2

V₄ I₁ H₄ U₁ I₁ O₁ O₁ 2nd Letter Triple

RACK 3

N₁ N₁ T₁ E₁ I₁ R₁ R₁

RACK 4

PAR SCORE 105-115   FOUR RACK TOTAL ════

26

U₁ L₁ P₃ K₅ T₁ C₃ O₁

RACK 1

A₁ T₁ T₁ T₁ Y₄ R₁ L₁ Triple Word Score

RACK 2

I₁ A₁ R₁ N₁ R₁ G₂ D₂ 3rd Letter Triple

RACK 3

U₁ C₃ F₄ L₁ T₁ A₁ A₁

RACK 4

PAR SCORE 105-115   FOUR RACK TOTAL ════

27

X_8	F_4	E_1	U_1	E_1	L_1	F_4	Double Word Score

RACK 1

D_2	P_3	A_1	A_1	U_1	P_3	L_1

RACK 2

N_1	S_1	B_3	N_1	A_1	O_1	U_1	Triple Word Score

RACK 3

E_1	O_1	O_1	I_1	I_1	L_1	R_1

RACK 4

PAR SCORE 90-100   FOUR RACK TOTAL ═══

28

R_1	L_1	Y_4	A_1	R_1	I_1	B_3

RACK 1

C_3	I_1	U_1	R_1	I_1	J_8	D_2

RACK 2

N_1	D_2	C_3	R_1	O_1	O_1	U_1	4th Letter Double

RACK 3

E_1	G_2	M_3	N_1	R_1	E_1	A_1

RACK 4

PAR SCORE 105-115   FOUR RACK TOTAL ═══

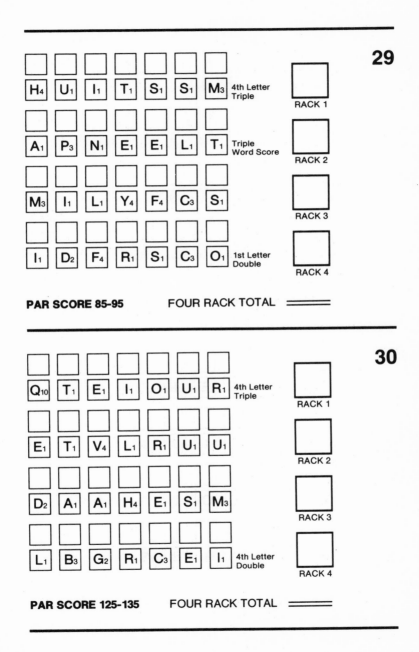

29

H₄	U₁	I₁	T₁	S₁	S₁	M₃	4th Letter Triple

RACK 1

| A₁ | P₃ | N₁ | E₁ | E₁ | L₁ | T₁ | Triple Word Score

RACK 2

| M₃ | I₁ | L₁ | Y₄ | F₄ | C₃ | S₁ |

RACK 3

| I₁ | D₂ | F₄ | R₁ | S₁ | C₃ | O₁ | 1st Letter Double

RACK 4

PAR SCORE 85-95   FOUR RACK TOTAL ════

30

| Q₁₀ | T₁ | E₁ | I₁ | O₁ | U₁ | R₁ | 4th Letter Triple

RACK 1

| E₁ | T₁ | V₄ | L₁ | R₁ | U₁ | U₁ |

RACK 2

| D₂ | A₁ | A₁ | H₄ | E₁ | S₁ | M₃ |

RACK 3

| L₁ | B₃ | G₂ | R₁ | C₃ | E₁ | I₁ | 4th Letter Double

RACK 4

PAR SCORE 125-135   FOUR RACK TOTAL ════

31

T₁	M₃	R₁	T₁	N₁	I₁	E₁

L₁	A₁	D₂	C₃	F₄	C₃	I₁	1st & 4th Letter Double

I₁	P₃	S₁	V₄	U₁	N₁	H₄	Double Word Score

E₁	Y₄	N₁	S₁	R₁	blank	E₁

RACK 1

RACK 2

RACK 3

RACK 4

PAR SCORE 115-125   FOUR RACK TOTAL ═══

32

A₁	R₁	U₁	G₂	E₁	P₃	D₂	4th Letter Triple

O₁	N₁	L₁	C₃	C₃	I₁	A₁

Y₄	V₄	B₃	E₁	T₁	R₁	I₁	4th Letter Double

H₄	L₁	F₄	I₁	L₁	I₁	R₁	Triple Word Score

RACK 1

RACK 2

RACK 3

RACK 4

PAR SCORE 155-165   FOUR RACK TOTAL ═══

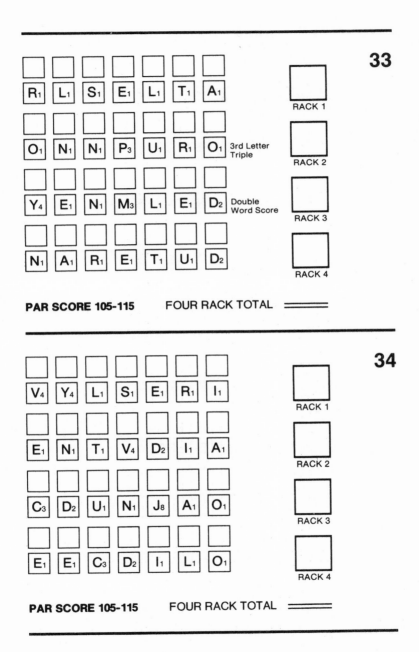

33

R₁	L₁	S₁	E₁	L₁	T₁	A₁

RACK 1

O₁	N₁	N₁	P₃	U₁	R₁	O₁

3rd Letter Triple

RACK 2

Y₄	E₁	N₁	M₃	L₁	E₁	D₂

Double Word Score

RACK 3

N₁	A₁	R₁	E₁	T₁	U₁	D₂

RACK 4

PAR SCORE 105-115   FOUR RACK TOTAL ═══

34

V₄	Y₄	L₁	S₁	E₁	R₁	I₁

RACK 1

E₁	N₁	T₁	V₄	D₂	I₁	A₁

RACK 2

C₃	D₂	U₁	N₁	J₈	A₁	O₁

RACK 3

E₁	E₁	C₃	D₂	I₁	L₁	O₁

RACK 4

PAR SCORE 105-115   FOUR RACK TOTAL ═══

35

U_1	Y_4	H_4	P_3	T_1	G_2	A_1

1st & 4th Letters Triple

RACK 1

O_1	L_1	R_1	A_1	B_3	N_1	Z_{10}

RACK 2

A_1	E_1	C_3	H_4	N_1	blank	K_5

Double Word Score

RACK 3

P_3	R_1	A_1	A_1	D_2	E_1	T_1

RACK 4

PAR SCORE 170-180   FOUR RACK TOTAL =====

36

E_1	T_1	B_3	L_1	I_1	T_1	R_1

RACK 1

I_1	X_8	O_1	R_1	E_1	F_4	A_1

3rd Letter Triple

RACK 2

A_1	L_1	A_1	G_2	N_1	I_1	M_3

Double Word Score

RACK 3

O_1	L_1	H_4	C_3	N_1	A_1	Y_4

RACK 4

PAR SCORE 125-135   FOUR RACK TOTAL =====

37

E₁	O₁	H₄	L₁	R₁	P₃	C₃

2nd & 4th Let-
ters Triple

RACK 1

B₃	R₁	B₃	R₁	R₁	E₁	A₁

RACK 2

A₁	E₁	A₁	G₂	R₁	E₁	V₄

RACK 3

O₁	R₁	P₃	N₁	L₁	I₁	U₁

Double
Word Score

RACK 4

PAR SCORE 110-120   FOUR RACK TOTAL ═══

38

L₁	A₁	R₁	T₁	E₁	A₁	B₃

RACK 1

R₁	N₁	L₁	A₁	E₁	A₁	O₁

RACK 2

E₁	E₁	I₁	I₁	D₂	D₂	F₄

1st & 4th Let-
ters Double

RACK 3

T₁	U₁	D₂	A₁	I₁	O₁	R₁

RACK 4

PAR SCORE 140-150   FOUR RACK TOTAL ═══

39

S_1	L_1	C_3	L_1	U_1	A_1	O_1	Triple Word Score

RACK 1

A_1	R_1	H_4	O_1	R_1	V_4	B_3

RACK 2

C_3	I_1	M_3	N_1	A_1	S_1	A_1	3rd Letter Triple

RACK 3

D_2	E_1	E_1	S_1	U_1	N_1	E_1	4th Letter Double

RACK 4

PAR SCORE 115–125   FOUR RACK TOTAL =====

40

H_4	R_1	B_3	N_1	T_1	A_1	C_3	Double Word Score

RACK 1

L_1	R_1	S_1	E_1	H_4	T_1	E_1

RACK 2

C_3	L_1	E_1	T_1	I_1	P_3	P_3	1st & 3rd Letters Double

RACK 3

L_1	blank	L_1	blank	O_1	O_1	A_1

RACK 4

PAR SCORE 115–125   FOUR RACK TOTAL =====

41

Y₄	B₃	W₄	E₁	E₁	R₁	R₁

RACK 1

N₁	K₅	R₁	H₄	E₁	G₂	I₁	2nd Letter Triple

RACK 2

U₁	O₁	U₁	A₁	C₃	S₁	R₁

RACK 3

L₁	L₁	S₁	E₁	T₁	Y₄	O₁	Triple Word Score

RACK 4

PAR SCORE 165-175   FOUR RACK TOTAL ═══

42

M₃	S₁	N₁	N₁	I₁	L₁	A₁	Triple Word Score

RACK 1

U₁	U₁	Y₄	L₁	Y₄	R₁	X₈

RACK 2

O₁	R₁	M₃	N₁	blank	A₁	E₁	3rd Letter Double

RACK 3

O₁	O₁	N₁	S₁	T₁	R₁	D₂

RACK 4

PAR SCORE 65-75   FOUR RACK TOTAL ═══

43

E_1	A_1	B_3	L_1	M_3	R_1	C_3	1st & 4th Letters Triple
E_1	U_1	N_1	A_1	R_1	I_1	I_1	
D_2	R_1	P_3	T_1	N_1	O_1	E_1	
U_1	H_4	W_4	S_1	T_1	A_1	O_1	4th Letter Triple

RACK 1

RACK 2

RACK 3

RACK 4

PAR SCORE 155-165   FOUR RACK TOTAL ═══

44

S_1	A_1	U_1	E_1	L_1	O_1	Z_{10}	
V_4	L_1	E_1	N_1	A_1	E_1	S_1	2nd Letter Double
R_1	G_2	U_1	L_1	E_1	O_1	B_3	3rd Letter Triple
E_1	I_1	A_1	W_4	P_3	L_1	H_4	

RACK 1

RACK 2

RACK 3

RACK 4

PAR SCORE 110-120   FOUR RACK TOTAL ═══

45

U₁	T₁	O₁	C₃	L₁	E₁	P₃

RACK 1

S₁	U₁	R₁	U₁	O₁	F₄	I₁	Triple Word Score

RACK 2

N₁	T₁	I₁	R₁	A₁	E₁	M₃

RACK 3

C₃	T₁	N₁	R₁	H₄	E₁	K₅	Double Word Score

RACK 4

PAR SCORE 165-175   FOUR RACK TOTAL ═══

46

Y₄	T₁	N₁	O₁	I₁	R₁	F₄	Triple Word Score

RACK 1

S₁	O₁	U₁	I₁	C₃	P₃	O₁	2nd Letter Triple

RACK 2

D₂	I₁	A₁	T₁	M₃	S₁	T₁

RACK 3

U₁	E₁	L₁	T₁	O₁	N₁	I₁

RACK 4

PAR SCORE 115-125   FOUR RACK TOTAL ═══

47

Y_4	G_2	U_1	Q_{10}	E_1	A_1	A_1	1st & 4th Letters Triple

RACK 1

K_5	P_3	L_1	P_3	R_1	R_1	O_1

RACK 2

A_1	R_1	V_4	T_1	N_1	L_1	E_1	1st Letter Double

RACK 3

A_1	D_2	X_8	H_4	T_1	E_1	T_1

RACK 4

PAR SCORE 90-100   FOUR RACK TOTAL ═══

48

L_1	R_1	D_2	U_1	E_1	I_1	B_3

RACK 1

C_3	T_1	L_1	C_3	I_1	A_1	A_1	3rd Letter Triple

RACK 2

S_1	M_3	L_1	R_1	A_1	I_1	E_1	Double Word Score

RACK 3

O_1	O_1	H_4	S_1	E_1	N_1	R_1	4th Letter Double

RACK 4

PAR SCORE 150-160   FOUR RACK TOTAL ═══

49

O₁	A₁	I₁	L₁	I₁	S₁	N₁

RACK 1

G₂	G₂	E₁	U₁	O₁	R₁	R₁

Double Word Score

RACK 2

I₁	N₁	L₁	C₃	A₁	O₁	D₂

3rd Letter Triple

RACK 3

U₁	E₁	S₁	T₁	S₁	S₁	I₁

RACK 4

PAR SCORE 140-150   FOUR RACK TOTAL ═══

50

G₂	B₃	E₁	M₃	A₁	O₁	R₁

3rd Letter Double

RACK 1

L₁	B₃	G₂	I₁	E₁	T₁	T₁

Triple Word Score

RACK 2

Y₄	L₁	A₁	L₁	E₁	G₂	R₁

RACK 3

P₃	H₄	E₁	S₁	N₁	E₁	R₁

RACK 4

PAR SCORE 115-125   FOUR RACK TOTAL ═══

51

T_1	S_1	M_3	M_3	E_1	I_1	I_1

E_1	S_1	W_4	P_3	R_1	I_1	I_1

1st & 4th Letters Triple

R_1	I_1	E_1	L_1	V_4	N_1	S_1

4th Letter Double

A_1	O_1	N_1	E_1	F_4	T_1	D_2

RACK 1

RACK 2

RACK 3

RACK 4

PAR SCORE 95–105   FOUR RACK TOTAL ═══

52

E_1	T_1	M_3	T_1	A_1	U_1	D_2

N_1	N_1	A_1	A_1	I_1	E_1	C_3

Double Word Score

N_1	E_1	G_2	L_1	D_2	I_1	J_8

4th Letter Double

G_2	R_1	U_1	T_1	E_1	N_1	H_4

RACK 1

RACK 2

RACK 3

RACK 4

PAR SCORE 95–105   FOUR RACK TOTAL ═══

53

N₁	F₄	R₁	I₁	A₁	F₄	U₁

RACK 1

L₁	A₁	T₁	A₁	E₁	P₃	C₃

4th Letter Triple

RACK 2

V₄	D₂	A₁	I₁	A₁	N₁	E₁

Triple Word Score

RACK 3

G₂	A₁	B₃	T₁	O₁	T₁	U₁

RACK 4

PAR SCORE 140–150   FOUR RACK TOTAL ═══

54

N₁	L₁	I₁	G₂	E₁	U₁	U₁

3rd Letter Double

RACK 1

R₁	C₃	V₄	T₁	O₁	I₁	I₁

Triple Word Score

RACK 2

I₁	N₁	M₃	E₁	E₁	L₁	H₄

RACK 3

Y₄	D₂	B₃	L₁	N₁	O₁	I₁

RACK 4

PAR SCORE 70–80   FOUR RACK TOTAL ═══

55

I₁	D₂	D₂	A₁	N₁	I₁	S₁

T₁	O₁	L₁	M₃	L₁	U₁	E₁

Double Word Score

E₁	G₂	S₁	U₁	R₁	L₁	G₂

2nd Letter Triple

M₃	F₄	P₃	R₁	U₁	E₁	E₁

RACK 1

RACK 2

RACK 3

RACK 4

PAR SCORE 125–135   FOUR RACK TOTAL ═══

56

T₁	C₃	O₁	L₁	R₁	I₁	S₁

I₁	T₁	S₁	A₁	E₁	L₁	R₁

I₁	T₁	H₄	T₁	Y₄	W₄	C₃

Triple Word Score

A₁	M₃	D₂	I₁	N₁	N₁	O₁

RACK 1

RACK 2

RACK 3

RACK 4

PAR SCORE 110–120   FOUR RACK TOTAL ═══

57

A₁	Y₄	O₁	H₄	R₁	T₁	E₁	Double Word Score

RACK 1

| L₁ | T₁ | R₁ | S₁ | T₁ | E₁ | A₁ |

RACK 2

| R₁ | N₁ | O₁ | P₃ | D₂ | P₃ | E₁ | 4th Letter Double

RACK 3

| R₁ | G₂ | R₁ | Y₄ | E₁ | B₃ | D₂ | 2nd Letter Triple

RACK 4

PAR SCORE 100-110   FOUR RACK TOTAL ═══

58

| S₁ | E₁ | U₁ | U₁ | M₃ | T₁ | M₃ | Double Word Score

RACK 1

| T₁ | U₁ | S₁ | C₃ | I₁ | B₃ | I₁ |

RACK 2

| U₁ | Y₄ | L₁ | H₄ | A₁ | S₁ | S₁ |

RACK 3

| R₁ | V₄ | E₁ | G₂ | L₁ | E₁ | O₁ | Double Word Score

RACK 4

PAR SCORE 70-80   FOUR RACK TOTAL ═══

59

T₁	I₁	B₃	S₁	E₁	S₁	U₁

RACK 1

R₁	H₄	A₁	K₅	W₄	A₁	E₁

1st Letter Triple

RACK 2

N₁	U₁	P₃	E₁	L₁	R₁	D₂

RACK 3

R₁	O₁	U₁	T₁	E₁	R₁	P₃

Triple Word Score

RACK 4

PAR SCORE 140-150   FOUR RACK TOTAL ═══

60

D₂	I₁	H₄	B₃	R₁	N₁	E₁

3rd Letter Double

RACK 1

O₁	M₃	I₁	I₁	I₁	N₁	N₁

Triple Word Score

RACK 2

E₁	U₁	B₃	D₂	M₃	S₁	E₁

RACK 3

R₁	V₄	I₁	E₁	O₁	L₁	I₁

RACK 4

PAR SCORE 70-80   FOUR RACK TOTAL ═══

61

S_1	T_1	I_1	T_1	E_1	A_1	H_4
A_1	C_3	O_1	E_1	O_1	L_1	R_1	Double Word Score
S_1	T_1	C_3	I_1	E_1	T_1	R_1
E_1	D_2	R_1	A_1	E_1	O_1	X_8	Triple Word Score

RACK 1

RACK 2

RACK 3

RACK 4

PAR SCORE 105-115   FOUR RACK TOTAL ══

62

E_1	O_1	T_1	I_1	L_1	N_1	V_4
E_1	T_1	R_1	F_4	E_1	I_1	L_1
R_1	R_1	U_1	I_1	C_3	S_1	E_1	2nd Letter Double
I_1	C_3	S_1	L_1	A_1	L_1	O_1

RACK 1

RACK 2

RACK 3

RACK 4

PAR SCORE 120-130   FOUR RACK TOTAL ══

63

Q_{10}	I_1	Y_4	I_1	R_1	N_1	U_1	Triple Word Score
E_1	T_1	R_1	I_1	D_2	P_3	I_1
I_1	A_1	C_3	H_4	T_1	O_1	B_3
P_3	E_1	L_1	M_3	B_3	I_1	E_1	4th Letter Double

RACK 1

RACK 2

RACK 3

RACK 4

PAR SCORE 155-165   FOUR RACK TOTAL ═══

64

E_1	L_1	H_4	S_1	E_1	S_1	V_4	3rd Letter Double
L_1	E_1	I_1	P_3	R_1	M_3	I_1
O_1	E_1	N_1	Y_4	I_1	R_1	F_4	Triple Word Score
I_1	O_1	N_1	N_1	L_1	O_1	U_1

RACK 1

RACK 2

RACK 3

RACK 4

PAR SCORE 100-110   FOUR RACK TOTAL ═══

65

H₄	F₄	S₁	O₁	I₁	I₁	Y₄

Triple Word Score

RACK 1

P₃	G₂	N₁	W₄	E₁	O₁	E₁

RACK 2

D₂	E₁	L₁	R₁	A₁	P₃	D₂

RACK 3

G₂	T₁	I₁	S₁	E₁	S₁	R₁

3rd Letter Double

RACK 4

PAR SCORE 105-115   FOUR RACK TOTAL =====

66

T₁	F₄	U₁	A₁	L₁	I₁	R₁

4th Letter Triple

RACK 1

P₃	R₁	S₁	L₁	W₄	R₁	A₁

RACK 2

D₂	E₁	I₁	N₁	T₁	A₁	S₁

RACK 3

B₃	O₁	N₁	N₁	A₁	O₁	B₃

RACK 4

PAR SCORE 55-65   FOUR RACK TOTAL =====

67

V_4	N_1	N_1	C_3	O_1	E_1	I_1

RACK 1

L_1	T_1	P_3	S_1	A_1	U_1	O_1

Double Word Score

RACK 2

D_2	O_1	A_1	R_1	I_1	E_1	V_4

Triple Word Score

RACK 3

D_2	S_1	C_3	blank	A_1	E_1	A_1

RACK 4

PAR SCORE 140-150 FOUR RACK TOTAL ===

68

R_1	V_4	G_2	Y_4	I_1	A_1	A_1

1st Letter Double

RACK 1

Z_{10}	D_2	O_1	I_1	I_1	E_1	X_8

Triple Word Score

RACK 2

O_1	R_1	F_4	L_1	G_2	T_1	O_1

RACK 3

O_1	Y_4	I_1	I_1	L_1	E_1	C_3

RACK 4

PAR SCORE 100-110 FOUR RACK TOTAL ===

69

C₃	S₁	A₁	R₁	L₁	T₁	H₄

RACK 1

S₁	I₁	E₁	T₁	O₁	S₁	R₁

RACK 2

G₂	E₁	T₁	O₁	N₁	T₁	C₃	Triple Word Score

RACK 3

E₁	E₁	E₁	E₁	N₁	V₄	R₁

RACK 4

PAR SCORE 70-80   FOUR RACK TOTAL ═══

70

P₃	T₁	R₁	O₁	F₄	O₁	O₁	1st Letter Double

RACK 1

Z₁₀	E₁	H₄	L₁	I₁	A₁	A₁

RACK 2

P₃	S₁	A₁	A₁	O₁	W₄	Y₄

RACK 3

O₁	I₁	T₁	T₁	T₁	R₁	C₃	Triple Word Score

RACK 4

PAR SCORE 70-80   FOUR RACK TOTAL ═══

71

C₃	E₁	Q₁₀	I₁	L₁	S₁	U₁

RACK 1

L₁	G₂	H₄	L₁	C₃	R₁	U₁

Double Word Score

RACK 2

L₁	F₄	A₁	A₁	A₁	blank	F₄

RACK 3

U₁	O₁	T₁	T₁	N₁	A₁	R₁

RACK 4

PAR SCORE 95-105   FOUR RACK TOTAL ═══

72

M₃	D₂	O₁	D₂	A₁	N₁	I₁

Triple Word Score

RACK 1

R₁	I₁	O₁	D₂	E₁	B₃	R₁

RACK 2

D₂	Y₄	O₁	I₁	O₁	blank	T₁

3rd Letter Double

RACK 3

T₁	T₁	Y₄	L₁	I₁	O₁	A₁

RACK 4

PAR SCORE 100-110   FOUR RACK TOTAL ═══

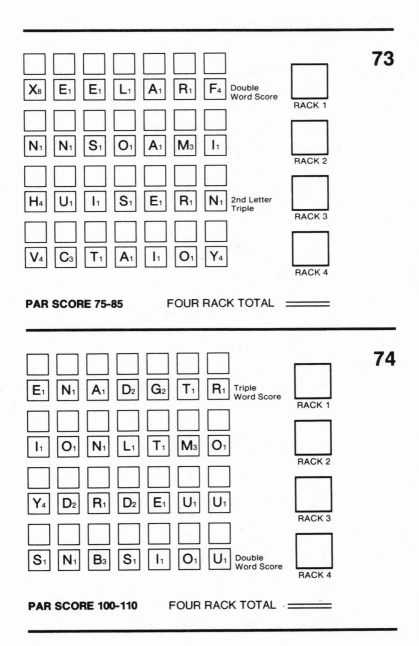

73

X₈	E₁	E₁	L₁	A₁	R₁	F₄

Double Word Score

RACK 1

N₁	N₁	S₁	O₁	A₁	M₃	I₁

RACK 2

H₄	U₁	I₁	S₁	E₁	R₁	N₁

2nd Letter Triple

RACK 3

V₄	C₃	T₁	A₁	I₁	O₁	Y₄

RACK 4

PAR SCORE 75-85   FOUR RACK TOTAL =====

74

E₁	N₁	A₁	D₂	G₂	T₁	R₁

Triple Word Score

RACK 1

I₁	O₁	N₁	L₁	T₁	M₃	O₁

RACK 2

Y₄	D₂	R₁	D₂	E₁	U₁	U₁

RACK 3

S₁	N₁	B₃	S₁	I₁	O₁	U₁

Double Word Score

RACK 4

PAR SCORE 100-110   FOUR RACK TOTAL =====

75

U₁	S₁	blank	S₁	C₃	S₁	E₁

Y₄	D₂	K₅	O₁	E₁	N₁	M₃	4th Letter Double

B₃	J₈	I₁	I₁	Y₄	A₁	G₂

S₁	F₄	I₁	N₁	I₁	U₁	O₁	1st Letter Triple

RACK 1

RACK 2

RACK 3

RACK 4

PAR SCORE 70-80   FOUR RACK TOTAL ═══

76

T₁	O₁	N₁	T₁	E₁	K₅	Y₄	Double Word Score

O₁	L₁	N₁	A₁	U₁	E₁	M₃	3rd Letter Triple

O₁	E₁	T₁	U₁	S₁	U₁	D₂

I₁	N₁	T₁	N₁	S₁	O₁	E₁

RACK 1

RACK 2

RACK 3

RACK 4

PAR SCORE 95-105   FOUR RACK TOTAL ═══

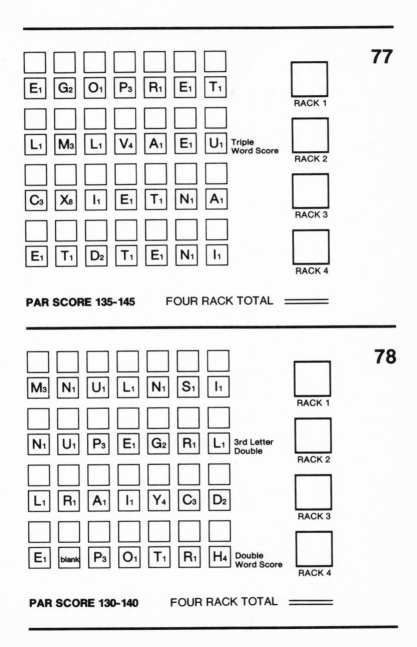

77

E₁	G₂	O₁	P₃	R₁	E₁	T₁
L₁	M₃	L₁	V₄	A₁	E₁	U₁ Triple Word Score
C₃	X₈	I₁	E₁	T₁	N₁	A₁
E₁	T₁	D₂	T₁	E₁	N₁	I₁

RACK 1
RACK 2
RACK 3
RACK 4

PAR SCORE 135-145   FOUR RACK TOTAL ====

78

M₃	N₁	U₁	L₁	N₁	S₁	I₁
N₁	U₁	P₃	E₁	G₂	R₁	L₁ 3rd Letter Double
L₁	R₁	A₁	I₁	Y₄	C₃	D₂
E₁	blank	P₃	O₁	T₁	R₁	H₄ Double Word Score

RACK 1
RACK 2
RACK 3
RACK 4

PAR SCORE 130-140   FOUR RACK TOTAL ====

79

L₁	S₁	T₁	U₁	I₁	M₃	R₁	Triple Word Score
Y₄	O₁	G₂	O₁	O₁	L₁	T₁
P₃	V₄	D₂	L₁	O₁	E₁	E₁
Z₁₀	R₁	B₃	I₁	E₁	E₁	A₁	Double Word Score

RACK 1

RACK 2

RACK 3

RACK 4

PAR SCORE 115-125   FOUR RACK TOTAL ═══

80

I₁	E₁	D₂	S₁	N₁	O₁	K₅
R₁	U₁	J₈	L₁	M₃	L₁	F₄	Double Word Score
Y₄	N₁	I₁	A₁	I₁	T₁	N₁
O₁	U₁	M₃	N₁	T₁	N₁	O₁

RACK 1

RACK 2

RACK 3

RACK 4

PAR SCORE 90-100   FOUR RACK TOTAL ═══

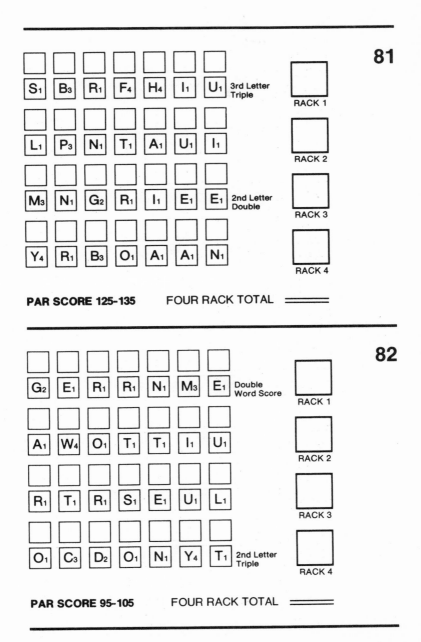

81

S₁	B₃	R₁	F₄	H₄	I₁	U₁	3rd Letter Triple

RACK 1

| L₁ | P₃ | N₁ | T₁ | A₁ | U₁ | I₁ |

RACK 2

| M₃ | N₁ | G₂ | R₁ | I₁ | E₁ | E₁ | 2nd Letter Double

RACK 3

| Y₄ | R₁ | B₃ | O₁ | A₁ | A₁ | N₁ |

RACK 4

PAR SCORE 125-135   FOUR RACK TOTAL ════

82

| G₂ | E₁ | R₁ | R₁ | N₁ | M₃ | E₁ | Double Word Score

RACK 1

| A₁ | W₄ | O₁ | T₁ | T₁ | I₁ | U₁ |

RACK 2

| R₁ | T₁ | R₁ | S₁ | E₁ | U₁ | L₁ |

RACK 3

| O₁ | C₃ | D₂ | O₁ | N₁ | Y₄ | T₁ | 2nd Letter Triple

RACK 4

PAR SCORE 95-105   FOUR RACK TOTAL ════

83

N_1	G_2	L_1	S_1	A_1	E_1	J_8	3rd Letter Double

RACK 1

D_2	L_1	N_1	H_4	A_1	F_4	U_1

RACK 2

H_4	T_1	E_1	C_3	D_2	I_1	A_1	Triple Word Score

RACK 3

A_1	I_1	E_1	T_1	E_1	R_1	P_3

RACK 4

PAR SCORE 115-125   FOUR RACK TOTAL =====

84

I_1	I_1	S_1	N_1	M_3	M_3	A_1	1st Letter Triple

RACK 1

T_1	A_1	A_1	I_1	E_1	S_1	B_3

RACK 2

C_3	R_1	L_1	L_1	N_1	I_1	Y_4	2nd Letter Triple

RACK 3

R_1	O_1	O_1	C_3	E_1	N_1	R_1

RACK 4

PAR SCORE 90-100   FOUR RACK TOTAL =====

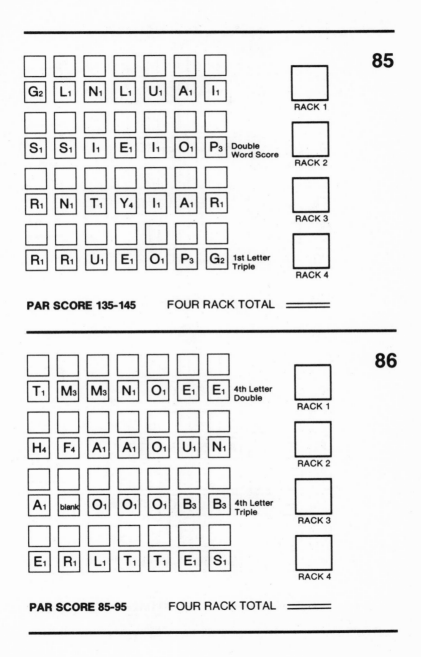

85

G₂	L₁	N₁	L₁	U₁	A₁	I₁

RACK 1

S₁	S₁	I₁	E₁	I₁	O₁	P₃	Double Word Score

RACK 2

R₁	N₁	T₁	Y₄	I₁	A₁	R₁

RACK 3

R₁	R₁	U₁	E₁	O₁	P₃	G₂	1st Letter Triple

RACK 4

PAR SCORE 135-145   FOUR RACK TOTAL ═══

86

T₁	M₃	M₃	N₁	O₁	E₁	E₁	4th Letter Double

RACK 1

H₄	F₄	A₁	A₁	O₁	U₁	N₁

RACK 2

A₁	blank	O₁	O₁	O₁	B₃	B₃	4th Letter Triple

RACK 3

E₁	R₁	L₁	T₁	T₁	E₁	S₁

RACK 4

PAR SCORE 85-95   FOUR RACK TOTAL ═══

87

E₁	A₁	L₁	I₁	Z₁₀	D₂	Y₄

1st Letter Double

RACK 1

T₁	N₁	O₁	A₁	O₁	E₁	C₃

RACK 2

G₂	G₂	U₁	U₁	E₁	I₁	O₁

RACK 3

Y₄	O₁	O₁	L₁	blank	E₁	G₂

RACK 4

PAR SCORE 90-100   FOUR RACK TOTAL ════

88

D₂	M₃	C₃	A₁	E₁	O₁	R₁

1st Letter Triple

RACK 1

E₁	E₁	N₁	A₁	N₁	P₃	T₁

RACK 2

R₁	E₁	A₁	I₁	L₁	C₃	R₁

2nd Letter Double

RACK 3

Y₄	L₁	I₁	O₁	K₅	J₈	L₁

Triple Word Score

RACK 4

PAR SCORE 155-165   FOUR RACK TOTAL ════

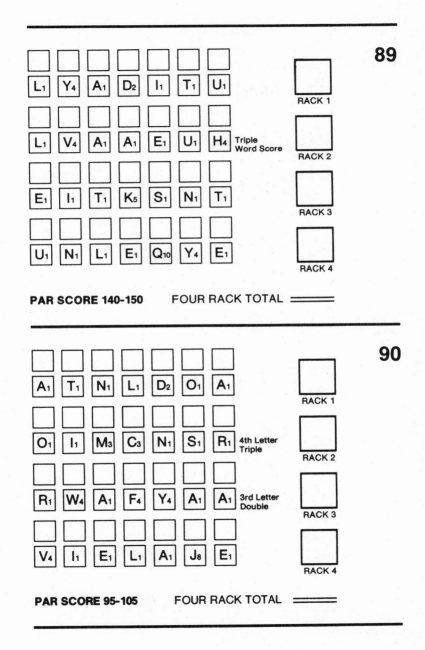

89

L₁	Y₄	A₁	D₂	I₁	T₁	U₁

RACK 1

L₁	V₄	A₁	A₁	E₁	U₁	H₄

Triple Word Score

RACK 2

E₁	I₁	T₁	K₅	S₁	N₁	T₁

RACK 3

U₁	N₁	L₁	E₁	Q₁₀	Y₄	E₁

RACK 4

PAR SCORE 140-150   FOUR RACK TOTAL ═══

90

A₁	T₁	N₁	L₁	D₂	O₁	A₁

RACK 1

O₁	I₁	M₃	C₃	N₁	S₁	R₁

4th Letter Triple

RACK 2

R₁	W₄	A₁	F₄	Y₄	A₁	A₁

3rd Letter Double

RACK 3

V₄	I₁	E₁	L₁	A₁	J₈	E₁

RACK 4

PAR SCORE 95-105   FOUR RACK TOTAL ═══

91

A_1	B_3	V_4	O_1	R_1	T_1	I_1	1st Letter Triple

RACK 1

O_1	F_4	T_1	D_2	N_1	L_1	E_1

RACK 2

I_1	B_3	H_4	A_1	O_1	N_1	Z_{10}	Double Word Score

RACK 3

A_1	R_1	E_1	I_1	P_3	P_3	E_1

RACK 4

PAR SCORE 100-110   FOUR RACK TOTAL =====

92

P_3	M_3	C_3	R_1	O_1	A_1	H_4

RACK 1

B_3	E_1	R_1	U_1	E_1	D_2	M_3	2nd Letter Triple

RACK 2

blank	Y_4	R_1	R_1	S_1	E_1	H_4

RACK 3

N_1	D_2	E_1	I_1	O_1	L_1	O_1	3rd Letter Triple

RACK 4

PAR SCORE 95-105   FOUR RACK TOTAL =====

93

R₁	A₁	O₁	I₁	E₁	M₃	P₃

4th Letter Double

RACK 1

A₁	E₁	S₁	L₁	O₁	T₁	C₃

RACK 2

A₁	T₁	H₄	L₁	C₃	N₁	N₁

Triple Word Score

RACK 3

R₁	N₁	H₄	D₂	R₁	U₁	I₁

Double Word Score

RACK 4

PAR SCORE 70-80   FOUR RACK TOTAL ═════

94

| U₁ | I₁ | F₄ | E₁ | L₁ | R₁ | A₁ |

RACK 1

| M₃ | S₁ | H₄ | I₁ | R₁ | L₁ | O₁ |

Double Word Score

RACK 2

| I₁ | J₈ | C₃ | N₁ | N₁ | O₁ | O₁ |

RACK 3

| L₁ | T₁ | N₁ | D₂ | B₃ | N₁ | O₁ |

1st Letter Triple

RACK 4

PAR SCORE 100-110   FOUR RACK TOTAL ═════

95

N_1	N_1	B_3	U_1	A_1	O_1	R_1	3rd Letter Double

RACK 1

N_1	A_1	O_1	V_4	O_1	T_1	I_1

RACK 2

G_2	N_1	E_1	R_1	A_1	T_1	T_1	3rd Letter Triple

RACK 3

X_8	E_1	L_1	O_1	R_1	L_1	C_3	3rd Letter Triple

RACK 4

PAR SCORE 70-80   FOUR RACK TOTAL ═══

96

N_1	R_1	W_4	G_2	L_1	E_1	O_1	4th Letter Triple

RACK 1

E_1	A_1	I_1	I_1	V_4	T_1	T_1

RACK 2

H_4	S_1	I_1	R_1	T_1	Y_4	M_3

RACK 3

E_1	W_4	R_1	A_1	U_1	U_1	K_5

RACK 4

PAR SCORE 65-75   FOUR RACK TOTAL ═══

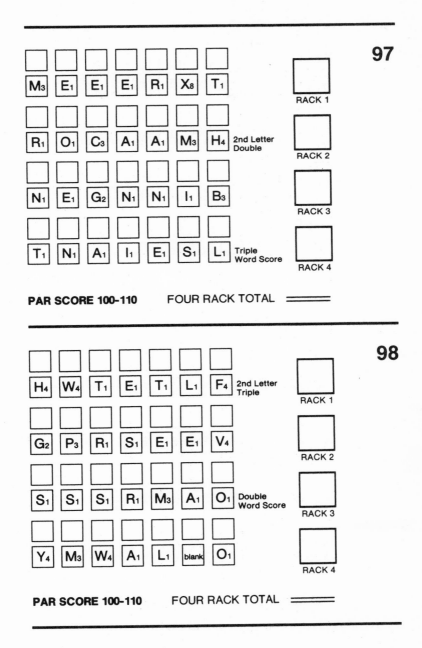

97

M₃ E₁ E₁ E₁ R₁ X₈ T₁

R₁ O₁ C₃ A₁ A₁ M₃ H₄ 2nd Letter Double

N₁ E₁ G₂ N₁ N₁ I₁ B₃

T₁ N₁ A₁ I₁ E₁ S₁ L₁ Triple Word Score

RACK 1
RACK 2
RACK 3
RACK 4

PAR SCORE 100-110   FOUR RACK TOTAL ═══

98

H₄ W₄ T₁ E₁ T₁ L₁ F₄ 2nd Letter Triple

G₂ P₃ R₁ S₁ E₁ E₁ V₄

S₁ S₁ S₁ R₁ M₃ A₁ O₁ Double Word Score

Y₄ M₃ W₄ A₁ L₁ blank O₁

RACK 1
RACK 2
RACK 3
RACK 4

PAR SCORE 100-110   FOUR RACK TOTAL ═══

99

A$_1$	I$_1$	C$_3$	T$_1$	M$_3$	E$_1$	L$_1$	1st Letter Double
N$_1$	E$_1$	K$_5$	C$_3$	O$_1$	A$_1$	B$_3$	Triple Word Score
E$_1$	L$_1$	U$_1$	M$_3$	O$_1$	I$_1$	I$_1$	
D$_2$	P$_3$	A$_1$	G$_2$	I$_1$	I$_1$	H$_4$	3rd Letter Triple

RACK 1

RACK 2

RACK 3

RACK 4

PAR SCORE 80-90   FOUR RACK TOTAL ═══

100

N$_1$	M$_3$	O$_1$	I$_1$	E$_1$	R$_1$	A$_1$	2nd Letter Triple
O$_1$	N$_1$	T$_1$	T$_1$	E$_1$	S$_1$	S$_1$	
U$_1$	C$_3$	R$_1$	E$_1$	P$_3$	O$_1$	I$_1$	3rd Letter Double
U$_1$	S$_1$	F$_4$	R$_1$	T$_1$	E$_1$	E$_1$	

RACK 1

RACK 2

RACK 3

RACK 4

PAR SCORE 85-95   FOUR RACK TOTAL ═══

101

R_1	O_1	T_1	I_1	L_1	D_2	R_1	Double Word Score
I_1	W_4	S_1	N_1	E_1	S_1	H_4
E_1	A_1	M_3	T_1	B_3	L_1	U_1	Triple Word Score
G_2	I_1	S_1	O_1	A_1	E_1	L_1

RACK 1

RACK 2

RACK 3

RACK 4

PAR SCORE 105-115   FOUR RACK TOTAL ====

102

V_4	O_1	U_1	N_1	L_1	E_1	S_1
E_1	R_1	blank	L_1	D_2	A_1	N_1	3rd Letter Triple
P_3	G_2	C_3	I_1	C_3	E_1	A_1	Double Word Score
R_1	D_2	A_1	T_1	B_3	E_1	E_1

RACK 1

RACK 2

RACK 3

RACK 4

PAR SCORE 95-105   FOUR RACK TOTAL ====

103

L_1	P_3	A_1	O_1	O_1	Y_4	G_2

S_1	L_1	F_4	H_4	O_1	I_1	O_1	Triple Word Score

B_3	E_1	J_8	R_1	S_1	U_1	I_1	1st Letter Double

H_4	T_1	S_1	E_1	C_3	K_5	A_1

RACK 1

RACK 2

RACK 3

RACK 4

PAR SCORE 120-130   FOUR RACK TOTAL ══

104

U_1	C_3	V_4	A_1	M_3	H_4	U_1	Triple Word Score

N_1	Z_{10}	S_1	S_1	E_1	E_1	E_1

A_1	S_1	M_3	R_1	H_4	I_1	A_1	Triple Word Score

T_1	I_1	N_1	U_1	S_1	E_1	G_2

RACK 1

RACK 2

RACK 3

RACK 4

PAR SCORE 85-95   FOUR RACK TOTAL ══

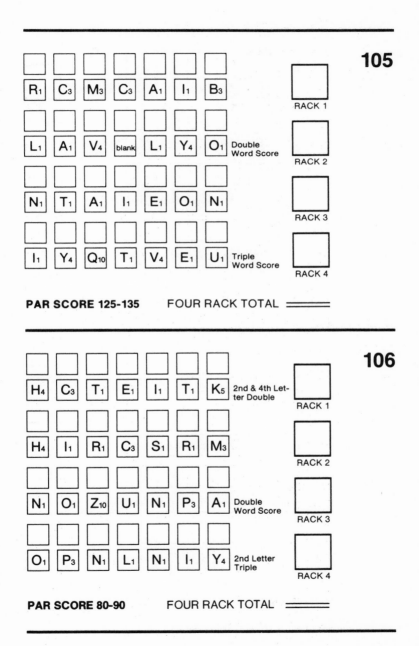

105

R₁	C₃	M₃	C₃	A₁	I₁	B₃

RACK 1

L₁	A₁	V₄	blank	L₁	Y₄	O₁

Double Word Score

RACK 2

N₁	T₁	A₁	I₁	E₁	O₁	N₁

RACK 3

I₁	Y₄	Q₁₀	T₁	V₄	E₁	U₁

Triple Word Score

RACK 4

PAR SCORE 125-135   FOUR RACK TOTAL ═══

106

H₄	C₃	T₁	E₁	I₁	T₁	K₅

2nd & 4th Letter Double

RACK 1

H₄	I₁	R₁	C₃	S₁	R₁	M₃

RACK 2

N₁	O₁	Z₁₀	U₁	N₁	P₃	A₁

Double Word Score

RACK 3

O₁	P₃	N₁	L₁	N₁	I₁	Y₄

2nd Letter Triple

RACK 4

PAR SCORE 80-90   FOUR RACK TOTAL ═══

107

Y₄	P₃	G₂	U₁	A₁	N₁	L₁

E₁	O₁	B₃	U₁	S₁	L₁	L₁

Triple Word Score

L₁	O₁	A₁	U₁	A₁	S₁	R₁

T₁	E₁	M₃	N₁	A₁	R₁	G₂

RACK 1

RACK 2

RACK 3

RACK 4

PAR SCORE 125-135   FOUR RACK TOTAL ═══

108

E₁	O₁	R₁	W₄	I₁	blank	O₁

3rd Letter Double

Y₄	R₁	C₃	E₁	S₁	L₁	I₁

T₁	A₁	T₁	N₁	L₁	B₃	A₁

Double Word Score

E₁	S₁	T₁	R₁	L₁	T₁	E₁

RACK 1

RACK 2

RACK 3

RACK 4

PAR SCORE 165-175   FOUR RACK TOTAL ═══

109

O$_1$	Y$_4$	F$_4$	L$_1$	L$_1$	I$_1$	M$_3$	2nd Letter Triple

RACK 1

| L$_1$ | E$_1$ | Z$_{10}$ | A$_1$ | L$_1$ | G$_2$ | E$_1$ | 3rd Letter Double |

RACK 2

| T$_1$ | V$_4$ | T$_1$ | I$_1$ | I$_1$ | A$_1$ | R$_1$ |

RACK 3

| Y$_4$ | N$_1$ | T$_1$ | N$_1$ | R$_1$ | O$_1$ | A$_1$ | 3rd Letter Triple |

RACK 4

PAR SCORE 105-115   FOUR RACK TOTAL ═══

110

| I$_1$ | R$_1$ | P$_3$ | D$_2$ | T$_1$ | A$_1$ | E$_1$ |

RACK 1

| E$_1$ | M$_3$ | L$_1$ | C$_3$ | U$_1$ | I$_1$ | Y$_4$ | 2nd Letter Triple |

RACK 2

| L$_1$ | T$_1$ | S$_1$ | I$_1$ | O$_1$ | R$_1$ | A$_1$ |

RACK 3

| R$_1$ | N$_1$ | C$_3$ | blank | S$_1$ | O$_1$ | U$_1$ |

RACK 4

PAR SCORE 135-145   FOUR RACK TOTAL ═══

111

O_1	A_1	N_1	Y_4	O_1	A_1	N_1	Double Word Score	RACK 1
M_3	S_1	N_1	D_2	I_1	I_1	U_1		RACK 2
C_3	T_1	L_1	A_1	I_1	E_1	T_1	3rd Letter Triple	RACK 3
R_1	K_5	H_4	N_1	E_1	S_1	U_1		RACK 4

PAR SCORE 95-105 FOUR RACK TOTAL

112

I_1	O_1	U_1	L_1	R_1	X_8	A_1	2nd Letter Triple	RACK 1
O_1	K_5	P_3	E_1	U_1	R_1	R_1		RACK 2
N_1	A_1	W_4	Y_4	M_3	L_1	O_1	Triple Word Score	RACK 3
U_1	G_2	D_2	O_1	L_1	N_1	H_4	2nd Letter Triple	RACK 4

PAR SCORE 125-135 FOUR RACK TOTAL

113

M₃	B₃	C₃	I₁	B₃	E₁	L₁

M₃ B₃ C₃ I₁ B₃ E₁ L₁ Triple Word Score

RACK 1

Y₄ S₁ J₈ R₁ E₁ E₁ T₁

RACK 2

T₁ L₁ D₂ A₁ E₁ F₄ E₁ 3rd Letter Double

RACK 3

H₄ H₄ N₁ P₃ T₁ A₁ A₁

RACK 4

PAR SCORE 110-120   FOUR RACK TOTAL ═══

114

A₁ N₁ O₁ S₁ B₃ U₁ R₁

RACK 1

H₄ W₄ A₁ E₁ R₁ S₁ E₁ 4th Letter Double

RACK 2

L₁ U₁ T₁ O₁ H₄ R₁ G₂ Double Word Score

RACK 3

blank Q₁₀ C₃ A₁ U₁ M₃ T₁ 2nd Letter Triple

RACK 4

PAR SCORE 70-80   FOUR RACK TOTAL ═══

115

T_1	S_1	B_3	M_3	U_1	U_1	E_1	4th Letter Triple

| A_1 | O_1 | T_1 | R_1 | G_2 | G_2 | A_1 |

| P_3 | A_1 | C_3 | A_1 | P_3 | L_1 | L_1 | Double Word Score |

| R_1 | R_1 | U_1 | N_1 | E_1 | O_1 | M_3 |

RACK 1
RACK 2
RACK 3
RACK 4

PAR SCORE 65-75   FOUR RACK TOTAL ═══

116

| N_1 | I_1 | H_4 | R_1 | I_1 | A_1 | P_3 | Triple Word Score |

| O_1 | I_1 | T_1 | N_1 | A_1 | E_1 | N_1 |

| T_1 | R_1 | P_3 | A_1 | N_1 | E_1 | O_1 |

| R_1 | C_3 | E_1 | E_1 | T_1 | O_1 | L_1 | 4th Letter Triple |

RACK 1
RACK 2
RACK 3
RACK 4

PAR SCORE 145-155   FOUR RACK TOTAL ═══

117

E_1	A_1	S_1	P_3	Y_4	L_1	R_1	3rd Letter Double

RACK 1

K_5	C_3	G_2	E_1	O_1	O_1	I_1	Triple Word Score

RACK 2

A_1	blank	L_1	H_4	N_1	E_1	C_3	

RACK 3

E_1	L_1	Y_4	blank	A_1	M_3	H_4	Double Word Score

RACK 4

PAR SCORE 150-160   FOUR RACK TOTAL ═══

118

E_1	E_1	E_1	V_4	G_2	N_1	R_1	2nd Letter Double

RACK 1

I_1	U_1	I_1	N_1	T_1	L_1	B_3	

RACK 2

T_1	P_3	N_1	N_1	O_1	O_1	O_1	

RACK 3

A_1	O_1	I_1	L_1	A_1	O_1	V_4	1st Letter Triple

RACK 4

PAR SCORE 125-135   FOUR RACK TOTAL ═══

119

P₃	R₁	T₁	O₁	O₁	R₁	E₁

A₁	S₁	Y₄	L₁	T₁	C₃	N₁	4th Letter Triple

O₁	O₁	T₁	I₁	S₁	D₂	U₁

R₁	L₁	R₁	J₈	V₄	K₅	U₁	Triple Word Score

RACK 1

RACK 2

RACK 3

RACK 4

PAR SCORE 95-105   FOUR RACK TOTAL =====

120

G₂	O₁	N₁	H₄	O₁	F₄	R₁	1st & 4th Letter Triple

Y₄	T₁	L₁	C₃	R₁	A₁	A₁

U₁	O₁	N₁	O₁	T₁	G₂	A₁	Double Word Score

O₁	I₁	A₁	N₁	N₁	W₄	T₁

RACK 1

RACK 2

RACK 3

RACK 4

PAR SCORE 100-110   FOUR RACK TOTAL =====

121

D₂	A₁	A₁	U₁	O₁	K₅	V₄

Triple Word Score

RACK 1

H₄	T₁	N₁	T₁	E₁	I₁	G₂

RACK 2

T₁	P₃	T₁	E₁	N₁	A₁	R₁

RACK 3

U₁	W₄	B₃	S₁	E₁	Y₄	N₁

Double Word Score

RACK 4

PAR SCORE 110-120   FOUR RACK TOTAL ══════

122

S₁	P₃	H₄	K₅	C₃	O₁	A₁

4th Letter Triple

RACK 1

E₁	N₁	N₁	T₁	T₁	X₈	A₁

RACK 2

Y₄	O₁	A₁	A₁	M₃	N₁	T₁

Double Word Score

RACK 3

M₃	A₁	O₁	I₁	U₁	C₃	R₁

RACK 4

PAR SCORE 105-115   FOUR RACK TOTAL ══════

123

O_1	S_1	S_1	S_1	R_1	I_1	C_3	1st Letter Triple
E_1	B_3	L_1	T_1	T_1	O_1	A_1	3rd Letter Double
H_4	S_1	E_1	E_1	T_1	Y_4	O_1	
K_5	N_1	A_1	N_1	Y_4	A_1	L_1	Double Word Score

RACK 1
RACK 2
RACK 3
RACK 4

PAR SCORE 95-105   FOUR RACK TOTAL ═══

124

Y_4	W_4	L_1	U_1	A_1	S_1	A_1	3rd Letter Triple
I_1	M_3	A_1	H_4	S_1	C_3	O_1	
M_3	F_4	I_1	O_1	E_1	L_1	A_1	Triple Word Score
L_1	R_1	blank	S_1	E_1	I_1	U_1	

RACK 1
RACK 2
RACK 3
RACK 4

PAR SCORE 105-115   FOUR RACK TOTAL ═══

125

R₁	I₁	E₁	Y₄	G₂	T₁	A₁

C₃	L₁	I₁	L₁	G₂	A₁	O₁

Double Word Score

E₁	E₁	A₁	L₁	P₃	T₁	R₁

U₁	C₃	S₁	Y₄	N₁	A₁	S₁

RACK 1

RACK 2

RACK 3

RACK 4

PAR SCORE 90-100   FOUR RACK TOTAL ═══

126

Q₁₀	U₁	U₁	N₁	I₁	E₁	A₁

4th Letter Triple

N₁	G₂	M₃	R₁	T₁	I₁	A₁

L₁	E₁	D₂	I₁	E₁	I₁	F₄

Double Word Score

A₁	O₁	C₃	N₁	T₁	D₂	E₁

RACK 1

RACK 2

RACK 3

RACK 4

PAR SCORE 75-85   FOUR RACK TOTAL ═══

127

I_1	O_1	S_1	N_1	blank	B_3	B_3	3rd Letter Triple

I_1	O_1	A_1	M_3	A_1	N_1	M_3

G_2	F_4	R_1	O_1	L_1	O_1	E_1

A_1	C_3	T_1	E_1	N_1	O_1	U_1	Triple Word Score

RACK 1

RACK 2

RACK 3

RACK 4

PAR SCORE 65-75   FOUR RACK TOTAL ═══

128

E_1	M_3	R_1	I_1	S_1	S_1	L_1	3rd Letter Triple

T_1	X_8	T_1	E_1	L_1	A_1	U_1	Triple Word Score

U_1	Y_4	V_4	R_1	E_1	S_1	O_1

N_1	U_1	D_2	O_1	S_1	Z_{10}	G_2	Triple Word Score

RACK 1

RACK 2

RACK 3

RACK 4

PAR SCORE 170-180   FOUR RACK TOTAL ═══

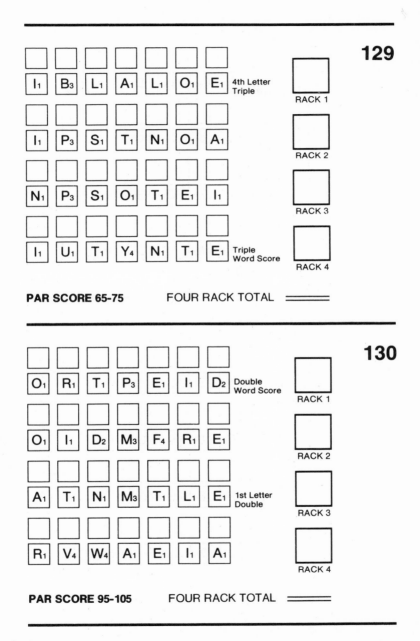

129

I₁	B₃	L₁	A₁	L₁	O₁	E₁	4th Letter Triple

I₁	P₃	S₁	T₁	N₁	O₁	A₁

N₁	P₃	S₁	O₁	T₁	E₁	I₁

I₁	U₁	T₁	Y₄	N₁	T₁	E₁	Triple Word Score

RACK 1
RACK 2
RACK 3
RACK 4

PAR SCORE 65-75   FOUR RACK TOTAL ═══

130

O₁	R₁	T₁	P₃	E₁	I₁	D₂	Double Word Score

O₁	I₁	D₂	M₃	F₄	R₁	E₁

A₁	T₁	N₁	M₃	T₁	L₁	E₁	1st Letter Double

R₁	V₄	W₄	A₁	E₁	I₁	A₁

RACK 1
RACK 2
RACK 3
RACK 4

PAR SCORE 95-105   FOUR RACK TOTAL ═══

131

X_8	F_4	F_4	R_1	I_1	E_1	O_1 3rd Letter Triple

RACK 1

E_1	R_1	G_2	D_2	I_1	T_1	I_1

RACK 2

T_1	O_1	S_1	E_1	A_1	O_1	G_2

RACK 3

U_1	Y_4	A_1	T_1	A_1	N_1	J_8 Triple Word Score

RACK 4

PAR SCORE 90-100   FOUR RACK TOTAL ═══

132

E_1	T_1	L_1	V_4	S_1	O_1	A_1

RACK 1

W_4	H_4	O_1	G_2	T_1	R_1	U_1 Double Word Score

RACK 2

N_1	Y_4	S_1	I_1	I_1	L_1	E_1

RACK 3

T_1	L_1	Y_4	U_1	Q_{10}	I_1	A_1 Triple Word Score

RACK 4

PAR SCORE 125-135   FOUR RACK TOTAL ═══

133

C₃	R₁	E₁	E₁	O₁	T₁	L₁

RACK 1

O₁	V₄	B₃	A₁	A₁	D₂	R₁	4th Letter Triple

RACK 2

K₅	C₃	A₁	U₁	P₃	T₁	B₃	Triple Word Score

RACK 3

T₁	E₁	P₃	I₁	Y₄	L₁	T₁

RACK 4

PAR SCORE 150-160   FOUR RACK TOTAL ═══

134

D₂	B₃	A₁	H₄	T₁	N₁	A₁

RACK 1

K₅	F₄	Y₄	E₁	A₁	B₃	R₁	Triple Word Score

RACK 2

A₁	E₁	L₁	N₁	A₁	C₃	P₃	Double Word Score

RACK 3

P₃	R₁	S₁	L₁	U₁	O₁	I₁

RACK 4

PAR SCORE 85-95   FOUR RACK TOTAL ═══

135

A_1	W_4	P_3	H_4	E_1	S_1	R_1	4th Letter Triple

RACK 1

A_1	R_1	I_1	E_1	E_1	T_1	T_1

RACK 2

O_1	E_1	Z_{10}	C_3	N_1	N_1	A_1	4th Letter Triple

RACK 3

T_1	A_1	O_1	N_1	I_1	S_1	Y_4

RACK 4

PAR SCORE 145-155   FOUR RACK TOTAL ═══

136

E_1	R_1	C_3	C_3	R_1	T_1	O_1

RACK 1

L_1	L_1	E_1	G_2	F_4	U_1	E_1

RACK 2

A_1	Y_4	R_1	M_3	T_1	R_1	O_1	Double Word Score

RACK 3

L_1	M_3	U_1	I_1	O_1	I_1	T_1	Double Word Score

RACK 4

PAR SCORE 135-145   FOUR RACK TOTAL ═══

137

D_2	N_1	F_4	Y_4	U_1	R_1	O_1

RACK 1

U_1	G_2	G_2	R_1	E_1	D_2	L_1 2nd Letter Triple

RACK 2

I_1	L_1	O_1	E_1	A_1	N_1	P_3 2nd Letter Double

RACK 3

Z_{10}	E_1	L_1	R_1	A_1	I_1	E_1 Triple Word Score

RACK 4

PAR SCORE 180-190   FOUR RACK TOTAL =====

138

C_3	L_1	S_1	I_1	I_1	A_1	A_1 Double Word Score

RACK 1

T_1	S_1	X_8	W_4	I_1	E_1	A_1

RACK 2

R_1	R_1	P_3	T_1	A_1	A_1	M_3

RACK 3

I_1	O_1	N_1	T_1	N_1	N_1	A_1

RACK 4

PAR SCORE 95-105   FOUR RACK TOTAL =====

139

I_1	O_1	S_1	F_4	N_1	S_1	I_1

RACK 1

L_1	I_1	A_1	M_3	T_1	R_1	P_3

4th Letter Triple

RACK 2

I_1	N_1	O_1	C_3	S_1	N_1	A_1

Double Word Score

RACK 3

T_1	R_1	H_4	L_1	U_1	C_3	T_1

RACK 4

PAR SCORE 60-70   FOUR RACK TOTAL ＝＝＝

140

M_3	I_1	A_1	C_3	I_1	U_1	L_1

1st Letter Triple

RACK 1

S_1	L_1	R_1	G_2	Y_4	S_1	A_1

RACK 2

E_1	S_1	H_4	R_1	R_1	F_4	E_1

3rd Letter Double

RACK 3

D_2	W_4	S_1	T_1	R_1	A_1	E_1

RACK 4

PAR SCORE 95-105   FOUR RACK TOTAL ＝＝＝

141

D₂	O₁	L₁	U₁	E₁	L₁	C₃

☐ RACK 1

A₁	O₁	S₁	I₁	T₁	M₃	R₁	2nd Letter Triple

☐ RACK 2

Y₄	O₁	C₃	O₁	R₁	E₁	K₅	Triple Word Score

☐ RACK 3

N₁	F₄	P₃	O₁	A₁	E₁	R₁

☐ RACK 4

PAR SCORE 180-190   FOUR RACK TOTAL ═══

142

B₃	T₁	N₁	L₁	H₄	M₃	U₁	Double Word Score

☐ RACK 1

A₁	N₁	C₃	E₁	E₁	T₁	U₁

☐ RACK 2

D₂	A₁	I₁	N₁	S₁	R₁	N₁

☐ RACK 3

X₈	P₃	O₁	I₁	R₁	L₁	A₁	Triple Word Score

☐ RACK 4

PAR SCORE 115-125   FOUR RACK TOTAL ═══

143

P₃	N₁	C₃	S₁	L₁	I₁	U₁

2nd Letter Double

E₁	L₁	U₁	T₁	S₁	G₂	I₁

E₁	I₁	V₄	A₁	L₁	I₁	G₂

Triple Word Score

M₃	E₁	L₁	B₃	E₁	T₁	M₃

RACK 1

RACK 2

RACK 3

RACK 4

PAR SCORE 100-110   FOUR RACK TOTAL ═══

144

E₁	E₁	R₁	E₁	L₁	K₅	N₁

N₁	G₂	O₁	E₁	A₁	O₁	R₁

4th Letter Triple

E₁	C₃	U₁	U₁	S₁	E₁	A₁

Double Word Score

E₁	A₁	I₁	T₁	E₁	N₁	R₁

RACK 1

RACK 2

RACK 3

RACK 4

PAR SCORE 120-130   FOUR RACK TOTAL ═══

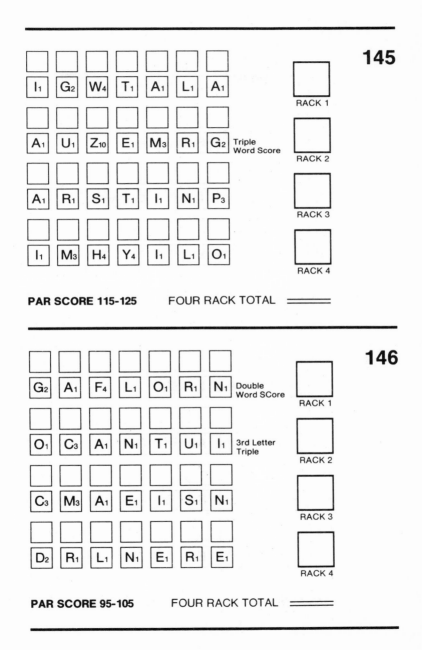

145

I₁	G₂	W₄	T₁	A₁	L₁	A₁

RACK 1

A₁	U₁	Z₁₀	E₁	M₃	R₁	G₂

Triple Word Score

RACK 2

A₁	R₁	S₁	T₁	I₁	N₁	P₃

RACK 3

I₁	M₃	H₄	Y₄	I₁	L₁	O₁

RACK 4

PAR SCORE 115-125   FOUR RACK TOTAL ═══

146

G₂	A₁	F₄	L₁	O₁	R₁	N₁

Double Word SCore

RACK 1

O₁	C₃	A₁	N₁	T₁	U₁	I₁

3rd Letter Triple

RACK 2

C₃	M₃	A₁	E₁	I₁	S₁	N₁

RACK 3

D₂	R₁	L₁	N₁	E₁	R₁	E₁

RACK 4

PAR SCORE 95-105   FOUR RACK TOTAL ═══

147

P_3	E_1	I_1	N_1	S_1	T_1	P_3	Double Word Score

O_1	L_1	H_4	T_1	S_1	I_1	D_2

I_1	Z_{10}	H_4	N_1	R_1	O_1	O_1	Triple Word Score

L_1	T_1	C_3	S_1	N_1	E_1	A_1

RACK 1

RACK 2

RACK 3

RACK 4

PAR SCORE 120-130   FOUR RACK TOTAL ══

148

N_1	I_1	Y_4	A_1	L_1	D_2	D_2

M_3	N_1	G_2	I_1	A_1	H_4	G_2

E_1	U_1	U_1	S_1	P_3	R_1	R_1	2nd Letter Double

E_1	N_1	A_1	A_1	L_1	T_1	V_4	3rd Letter Triple

RACK 1

RACK 2

RACK 3

RACK 4

PAR SCORE 125-135   FOUR RACK TOTAL ══

149

D₂	I₁	W₄	E₁	N₁	N₁	L₁	3rd Letter Triple

RACK 1

U₁	E₁	F₄	O₁	N₁	R₁	R₁	

RACK 2

L₁	M₃	A₁	A₁	I₁	L₁	X₈	Double Word Score

RACK 3

R₁	E₁	O₁	E₁	I₁	T₁	V₄	2nd Letter Double

RACK 4

PAR SCORE 105-115   FOUR RACK TOTAL ═══

150

A₁	P₃	D₂	S₁	M₃	I₁	H₄	2nd Letter Triple

RACK 1

O₁	L₁	S₁	L₁	P₃	O₁	C₃	

RACK 2

T₁	N₁	C₃	W₄	T₁	E₁	H₄	4th Letter Double

RACK 3

R₁	Y₄	N₁	G₂	U₁	O₁	I₁	

RACK 4

PAR SCORE 95-105   FOUR RACK TOTAL ═══

Solutions

1

E₁	A₁	R₁	M₃	U₁	F₄	F₄	RACK 1 = **71**
A₁	Z₁₀	O₁	T₁	H₄			RACK 2 = **34**
L₁	I₁	N₁	E₁	A₁	T₁	E₁	RACK 3 = **57**
S₁	N₁	U₁	G₂	L₁	Y₄		RACK 4 = **30**

PAR SCORE 140-150   JUDD'S TOTAL   **192**

2

D₂	E₁	V₄	I₁	A₁	T₁	E₁	RACK 1 = **83**
A₁	W₄	E₁	I₁	G₂	H₄		RACK 2 = **26**
P₃	O₁	P₃	G₂	U₁	N₁		RACK 3 = **11**
F₄	A₁	I₁	N₁	T₁	L₁	Y₄	RACK 4 = **63**

PAR SCORE 120-130   JUDD'S TOTAL   **183**

3

H₄	A₁	D₂	D₂	O₁	C₃	K₅	RACK 1 = **68**
C₃	E₁	R₁	T₁	A₁	I₁	N₁	RACK 2 = **59**
P₃	U₁	L₁	S₁	E₁	R₁		RACK 3 = **16**
N₁	E₁	X₈	U₁	S₁			RACK 4 = **36**

PAR SCORE 130-140   JUDD'S TOTAL   **179**

4

P₃	E₁	R₁	I₁	G₂	O₁	N₁	RACK 1 **66**
G₂	H₄	A₁	S₁	T₁	L₁	Y₄	RACK 2 **64**
M₃	I₁	L₁	K₅	E₁	R₁		RACK 3 - **24**
R₁	O₁	G₂	U₁	E₁			RACK 4 = **6**

PAR SCORE 115-125   JUDD'S TOTAL   **160**

5

G₂	E₁	R₁	U₁	N₁	D₂		RACK 1 - **16**
S₁	E₁	A₁	F₄	O₁	O₁	D₂	RACK 2 - **69**
V₄	A₁	R₁	I₁	E₁	D₂		RACK 3 = **10**
D₂	E₁	S₁	P₃	O₁	T₁		RACK 4 = **12**

PAR SCORE 75-85   JUDD'S TOTAL   **107**

6

F blank	I₁	F₄	T₁	E₁	E₁	N₁	RACK 1 = **59**
G₂	O₁	S₁	L₁	I₁	N₁	G₂	RACK 2 = **59**
H₄	E₁	R₁	E₁	I₁	N₁		RACK 3 = **27**
S₁	C₃	U₁	R₁	V₄	Y₄		RACK 4 = **42**

PAR SCORE 135-145   JUDD'S TOTAL   **187**

7
R₁ E₁ A₁ L₁ T₁ Y₄ — RACK 1 = **9**
N₁ A₁ T₁ U₁ R₁ A₁ L₁ — RACK 2 = **64**
L₁ A₁ R₁ Y₄ N₁ X₈ — RACK 3 = **16**
E₁ F₄ F₄ O₁ R₁ T₁ S₁ — RACK 4 = **63**
PAR SCORE 110-120   JUDD'S TOTAL **152**

8
F₄ L₁ O₁ T₁ S₁ A₁ M₃ — RACK 1 = **66**
B₃ E₁ N₁ E₁ A₁ T₁ H₄ — RACK 2 = **62**
A₁ S₁ T₁ R₁ A₁ Y₄ — RACK 3 = **18**
E₁ X₈ E₁ M₃ P₃ T₁ — RACK 4 = **17**
PAR SCORE 115-125   JUDD'S TOTAL **163**

9
N₁ E₁ P₃ H₄ E₁ W₄ — RACK 1 = **22**
L₁ I₁ K₅ E₁ L₁ Y₄ — RACK 2 = **13**
J₈ U₁ S₁ T₁ I₁ C₃ E₁ — RACK 3 = **82**
F₄ A₁ C₃ A₁ D₂ E₁ — RACK 4 = **12**
PAR SCORE 90-100   JUDD'S TOTAL **129**

10
I₁ N₁ F₄ I₁ D₂ E₁ L₁ — RACK 1 = **83**
M₃ A₁ N₁ G₂ E₁ — RACK 2 = **11**
A₁ U₁ R₁ I₁ C₃ L₁ E₁ — RACK 3 = **59**
S₁ T₁ A₁ T₁ U₁ S₁ — RACK 4 = **6**
PAR SCORE 120-130   JUDD'S TOTAL **159**

11
B₃ O₁ D₂ K₅ I₁ N₁ — RACK 1 = **23**
G₂ E₁ R₁ M₃ A₁ N₁ E₁ — RACK 2 = **60**
N₁ E₁ E₁ D₂ L₁ E₁ R₁ — RACK 3 = **58**
S₁ E₁ A₁ S₁ I₁ C₃ K(blank) — RACK 4 = **66**
PAR SCORE 150-160   JUDD'S TOTAL **207**

12
V₄ I₁ A₁ D₂ U₁ C₃ T₁ — RACK 1 = **63**
S₁ U₁ B₃ D₂ U₁ E₁ D₂ — RACK 2 = **61**
T₁ O₁ U₁ R₁ I₁ S₁ T₁ — RACK 3 = **57**
P₃ O₁ T₁ H₄ E₁ R₁ B₃ — RACK 4 = **64**
PAR SCORE 175-185   JUDD'S TOTAL **245**

13
S₁ E₁ R₁ E₁ N₁ E₁ — RACK 1 = **18**
E₁ N₁ T₁ O₁ M₃ B₃ S₁ — RACK 2 = **72**
C₃ O₁ N₁ D₂ U₁ I₁ T₁ — RACK 3 = **80**
N₁ E₁ A₁ R₁ B₃ Y₄ — RACK 4 = **11**
PAR SCORE 130-140   JUDD'S TOTAL **181**

14
A₁ R₁ D₂ U₁ O₁ U₁ S₁ — RACK 1 = **59**
B₃ O₁ O₁ S₁ T₁ E₁ R₁ — RACK 2 = **59**
D₂ R₁ E₁ D₂ G₂ E₁ — RACK 3 = **9**
P₃ E₁ E₁ L₁ E₁ R(blank) S₁ — RACK 4 = **58**
PAR SCORE 135-145   JUDD'S TOTAL **185**

15
K₅ L₁ A₁ X₈ O₁ N₁ — RACK 1 = **33**
P₃ L₁ U₁ N₁ G₂ E₁ — RACK 2 = **9**
A₁ U₁ T₁ O₁ P₃ S₁ Y₄ — RACK 3 = **64**
C₃ O₁ R₁ N₁ E₁ T₁ — RACK 4 = **8**
PAR SCORE 80-90   JUDD'S TOTAL **114**

16
I₁ G₂ N₁ O₁ B₃ L₁ E₁ — RACK 1 = **60**
S₁ T₁ A₁ R₁ K₅ — RACK 2 = **27**
C₃ R₁ U₁ E₁ L₁ T₁ Y₄ — RACK 3 = **62**
P₃ O₁ R₁ T₁ A₁ L₁ — RACK 4 = **8**
PAR SCORE 95-105   JUDD'S TOTAL **157**

17

S_1 T_1 E_1 P_3 S_1 O_1 N_1	RACK 1 =	**59**

S_1 T_1 E_1 P_3 S_1 O_1 N_1 — RACK 1 = **59**
G_2 L_1 O_1 R_1 Y_4 — RACK 2 = **18**
C_3 O_1 N_1 D_2 E_1 M_3 N_1 — RACK 3 = **86**
Z_{10} O_1 M_3 B_3 I_1 E_1 — RACK 4 = **19**
PAR SCORE 130-140 JUDD'S TOTAL **182**

18

C_3 O_1 R_1 R_1 O_1 D_2 E_1 — RACK 1 = **62**
P_3 A_1 T_1 S_1 Y_4 — RACK 2 = **20**
D_2 U_1 T_1 Y_4 — RACK 3 = **8**
V_4 I_1 O_1 L_1 I_1 N_1 — RACK 4 = **9**
PAR SCORE 70-80 JUDD'S TOTAL **99**

19

L_1 Y_4 M_3 P_3 H_4 — RACK 1 = **19**
H_4 E_1 C_3 T_1 A_1 R_1 E_1 — RACK 2 = **68**
B_3 O_1 A_1 T_1 E_1 R_1 — RACK 3 = **8**
A_1 S_1 T_1 I_1 R_1 — RACK 4 = **5**
PAR SCORE 70-80 JUDD'S TOTAL **100**

20

T_1 R_1 U_1 A_1 N_1 C_3 Y_4 — RACK 1 = **86**
P_3 A_1 S_1 T_1 E_1 R_1 N_1 — RACK 2 = **59**
C_3 Y_4 G_2 N_1 E_1 T_1 — RACK 3 = **20**
P_3 A_1 V_4 E_1 S_1 — RACK 4 = **10**
PAR SCORE 125-135 JUDD'S TOTAL **175**

21

P_3 E_1 R_1 P_3 L_1 E_1 X_8 — RACK 1 = **86**
D_2 R_1 U_1 N_1 K_5 — RACK 2 = **20**
A_1 R_1 M_3 O_1 R_1 Y_4 — RACK 3 = **11**
V_4 I_1 A_1 B_3 L_1 E_1 — RACK 4 = **17**
PAR SCORE 95-105 JUDD'S TOTAL **134**

22

D_2 I_1 L_1 U_1 T_1 E_1 — RACK 1 = **7**
S_1 H_4 O_1 W_4 N_1 — RACK 2 = **19**
G_2 I_1 Z_{10} M_3 O_1 — RACK 3 = **37**
L_1 E_1 C_3 T_1 E_1 R_1 N_1 — RACK 4 = **59**
PAR SCORE 85-95 JUDD'S TOTAL **122**

23

M_3 A_1 G_2 N_1 E_1 T_1 O_1 — RACK 1 = **60**
J_8 A_1 P_3 E_1 R_1 Y_4 — RACK 2 = **34**
K_5 N_1 I_1 F_4 E_1 R_1 — RACK 3 = **13**
R_1 I_1 D_2 D_2 L_1 E_1 S_1 — RACK 4 = **59**
PAR SCORE 120-130 JUDD'S TOTAL **166**

24

T_1 U_1 N_1 A_1 B_3 L_1 E_1 — RACK 1 = **61**
M_3 O_1 R_1 S_1 E_1 L_1 — RACK 2 = **16**
C_3 E_1 L_1 L_1 I_1 S_1 T_1 — RACK 3 = **59**
D_2 I_1 A_1 R_1 Y_4 — RACK 4 = **27**
PAR SCORE 115-125 JUDD'S TOTAL **163**

25

A_1 L_1 G_2 E_1 B_3 R_1 A_1 — RACK 1 = **64**
F_4 L_1 A_1 N_1 N_1 E_1 L_1 — RACK 2 = **60**
O_1 H_4 O_1 — RACK 3 = **14**
I_1 N_1 T_1 E_1 R_1 N_1 — RACK 4 = **6**
PAR SCORE 105-115 JUDD'S TOTAL **144**

26

P_3 O_1 T_1 L_1 U_1 C_3 K_5 — RACK 1 = **65**
T_1 A_1 R_1 T_1 L_1 Y_4 — RACK 2 = **27**
N_1 A_1 D_2 I_1 R_1 — RACK 3 = **10**
F_4 A_1 C_3 T_1 U_1 A_1 L_1 — RACK 4 = **62**
PAR SCORE 105-115 JUDD'S TOTAL **164**

27

E₁	F₄	F₄	L₁	U₁	X₈		RACK 1 = **38**
A₁	P₃	P₃	L₁	A₁	U₁	D₂	RACK 2 = **62**
B₃	O₁	S₁	U₁	N₁			RACK 3 = **21**
O₁	R₁	I₁	O₁	L₁	E₁		RACK 4 = **6**

PAR SCORE 90-100 JUDD'S TOTAL **127**

28

L₁	I₁	B₃	R₁	A₁	R₁	Y₄	RACK 1 = **62**
J₈	U₁	R₁	I₁	D₂	I₁	C₃	RACK 2 = **67**
C₃	O₁	R₁	D₂	O₁	N₁		RACK 3 = **11**
M₃	A₁	N₁	G₂	E₁	R₁		RACK 4 = **9**

PAR SCORE 105-115 JUDD'S TOTAL **149**

29

I₁	S₁	T₁	H₄	M₃	U₁	S₁	RACK 1 = **70**
P₃	L₁	A₁	N₁	E₁	T₁		RACK 2 = **24**
F₄	L₁	I₁	M₃	S₁	Y₄		RACK 3 = **14**
F₄	I₁	D₂	S₁				RACK 4 = **12**

PAR SCORE 85-95 JUDD'S TOTAL **120**

30

T₁	O₁	R₁	Q₁₀	U₁	E₁		RACK 1 = **35**
V₄	U₁	L₁	T₁	U₁	R₁	E₁	RACK 2 = **60**
A₁	S₁	H₄	A₁	M₃	E₁	D₂	RACK 3 = **63**
G₂	E₁	R₁	B₃	I₁	L₁		RACK 4 = **12**

PAR SCORE 125-135 JUDD'S TOTAL **170**

31

M₃	I₁	T₁	T₁	E₁	N₁		RACK 1 = **8**
F₄	L₁	A₁	C₃	C₃	I₁	D₂	RACK 2 = **72**
P₃	U₁	N₁	I₁	S₁	H₄		RACK 3 = **22**
S₁	C(blank)	E₁	N₁	E₁	R₁	Y₄	RACK 4 = **59**

PAR SCORE 115-125 JUDD'S TOTAL **161**

32

U₁	P₃	G₂	R₁	A₁	D₂	E₁	RACK 1 = **63**
L₁	A₁	C₃	O₁	N₁	I₁	C₃	RACK 2 = **61**
B₃	R₁	E₁	V₄	I₁	T₁	Y₄	RACK 3 = **69**
F₄	R₁	I₁	L₁	L₁			RACK 4 = **24**

PAR SCORE 155-165 JUDD'S TOTAL **217**

33

S₁	T₁	E₁	L₁	L₁	A₁	R₁	RACK 1 = **57**
P₃	R₁	O₁	N₁	O₁	U₁	N₁	RACK 2 = **61**
M₃	E₁	D₂	L₁	E₁	Y₄		RACK 3 = **24**
A₁	R₁	D₂	E₁	N₁	T₁		RACK 4 = **7**

PAR SCORE 105-115 JUDD'S TOTAL **149**

34

S₁	I₁	L₁	V₄	E₁	R₁	Y₄	RACK 1 = **63**
D₂	E₁	V₄	I₁	A₁	N₁	T₁	RACK 2 = **61**
J₈	O₁	C₃	U₁	N₁	D₂		RACK 3 = **16**
D₂	O₁	C₃	I₁	L₁	E₁		RACK 4 = **9**

PAR SCORE 105-115 JUDD'S TOTAL **149**

35

P₃	A₁	U₁	G₂	H₄	T₁	Y₄	RACK 1 = **76**
B₃	L₁	A₁	Z₁₀	O₁	N₁		RACK 2 = **17**
H₄	A₁	C₃	K₅	N₁	E₁	Y(blank)	RACK 3 = **80**
A₁	D₂	A₁	P₃	T₁	E₁	R₁	RACK 4 = **60**

PAR SCORE 170-180 JUDD'S TOTAL **233**

36

B₃	R₁	I₁	T₁	T₁	L₁	E₁	RACK 1 = **59**
F₄	O₁	X₈	I₁	E₁	R₁		RACK 2 = **32**
M₃	A₁	L₁	I₁	G₂	N₁		RACK 3 = **18**
H₄	A₁	L₁	C₃	Y₄	O₁	N₁	RACK 4 = **65**

PAR SCORE 125-135 JUDD'S TOTAL **174**

37

E₁ P₃ O₁ C₃ H₄ ▢ ▢ RACK 1 = **24**

B₃ A₁ R₁ B₃ E₁ R₁ ▢ RACK 2 = **10**

A₁ V₄ E₁ R₁ A₁ G₂ E₁ RACK 3 = **61**

P₃ U₁ R₁ L₁ O₁ I₁ N₁ RACK 4 = **68**

PAR SCORE 110-120   JUDD'S TOTAL   **163**

38

R₁ A₁ T₁ A₁ B₃ L₁ E₁ RACK 1 = **59**

L₁ O₁ A₁ N₁ E₁ R₁ ▢ RACK 2 = **6**

D₂ E₁ I₁ F₄ I₁ E₁ D₂ RACK 3 = **68**

A₁ U₁ D₂ I₁ T₁ O₁ R₁ RACK 4 = **58**

PAR SCORE 140-150   JUDD'S TOTAL   **191**

39

C₃ A₁ L₁ L₁ O₁ U₁ S₁ RACK 1 = **77**

H₄ A₁ R₁ B₃ O₁ R₁ ▢ RACK 2 = **11**

M₃ A₁ N₁ I₁ A₁ C₃ S₁ RACK 3 = **63**

S₁ U₁ E₁ D₂ E₁ ▢ ▢ RACK 4 = **8**

PAR SCORE 115-125   JUDD'S TOTAL   **159**

40

B₃ R₁ A₁ N₁ C₃ H₄ ▢ RACK 1 = **26**

S₁ H₄ E₁ L₁ T₁ E₁ R₁ RACK 2 = **60**

P₃ E₁ P₃ T₁ I₁ C₃ RACK 3 = **18**

A₁ L₁ C(blank) O₁ H(blank) O₁ L₁ RACK 4 = **55**

PAR SCORE 115-125   JUDD'S TOTAL   **159**

41

B₃ R₁ E₁ W₄ E₁ R₁ Y₄ RACK 1 = **65**

G₂ H₄ E₁ R₁ K₅ I₁ N₁ RACK 2 = **73**

R₁ A₁ U₁ C₃ O₁ U₁ S₁ RACK 3 = **59**

S₁ O₁ L₁ E₁ L₁ Y₄ RACK 4 = **27**

PAR SCORE 165-175   JUDD'S TOTAL   **224**

42

N₁ A₁ N₁ I₁ S₁ M₃ ▢ RACK 1 = **24**

L₁ U₁ X₈ U₁ R₁ Y₄ ▢ RACK 2 = **16**

A₁ N₁ Y(blank) M₃ O₁ R₁ E₁ RACK 3 = **58**

D₂ O₁ N₁ O₁ R₁ S₁ ▢ RACK 4 = **7**

PAR SCORE 65-75   JUDD'S TOTAL   **105**

43

C₃ L₁ A₁ M₃ B₃ E₁ R₁ RACK 1 = **75**

R₁ A₁ I₁ N₁ ▢ ▢ ▢ RACK 2 = **4**

P₃ O₁ R₁ T₁ E₁ N₁ D₂ RACK 3 = **60**

W₄ A₁ S₁ H₄ O₁ U₁ T₁ RACK 4 = **71**

PAR SCORE 155-165   JUDD'S TOTAL   **210**

44

Z₁₀ E₁ A₁ L₁ O₁ U₁ S₁ RACK 1 = **66**

E₁ N₁ S₁ L₁ A₁ V₄ E₁ RACK 2 = **61**

B₃ U₁ G₂ L₁ E₁ R₁ ▢ RACK 3 = **13**

A₁ W₄ H₄ I₁ L₁ E₁ ▢ RACK 4 = **12**

PAR SCORE 110-120   JUDD'S TOTAL   **152**

45

C₃ O₁ U₁ P₃ L₁ E₁ T₁ RACK 1 = **61**

F₄ U₁ R₁ I₁ O₁ U₁ S₁ RACK 2 = **80**

R₁ A₁ I₁ M₃ E₁ N₁ T₁ RACK 3 = **59**

K₅ E₁ T₁ C₃ H₄ ▢ ▢ RACK 4 = **28**

PAR SCORE 165-175   JUDD'S TOTAL   **228**

46

N₁ O₁ T₁ I₁ F₄ Y₄ ▢ RACK 1 = **36**

C₃ O₁ P₃ I₁ O₁ U₁ S₁ RACK 2 = **63**

A₁ M₃ I₁ D₂ S₁ T₁ ▢ RACK 3 = **9**

O₁ U₁ T₁ L₁ I₁ N₁ E₁ RACK 4 = **57**

PAR SCORE 115-125   JUDD'S TOTAL   **165**

47
Q₁₀ U₁ A₁ Y₄ A₁ G₂ E₁ RACK 1 = **98**
P₃ O₁ R₁ K₅ ☐ ☐ RACK 2 = **10**
V₄ E₁ R₁ N₁ A₁ L₁ RACK 3 = **13**
H₄ E₁ X₈ A₁ D₂ ☐ ☐ RACK 4 = **16**
PAR SCORE 90-100   JUDD'S TOTAL **137**

48
B₃ U₁ I₁ L₁ D₂ E₁ R₁ RACK 1 = **60**
L₁ A₁ C₃ T₁ I₁ C₃ RACK 2 = **16**
R₁ E₁ A₁ L₁ I₁ S₁ M₃ RACK 3 = **68**
O₁ N₁ S₁ H₄ O₁ R₁ E₁ RACK 4 = **64**
PAR SCORE 150-160   JUDD'S TOTAL **208**

49
L₁ I₁ A₁ I₁ S₁ O₁ N₁ RACK 1 = **57**
G₂ O₁ U₁ G₂ E₁ R₁ RACK 2 = **16**
N₁ O₁ D₂ I₁ C₃ A₁ L₁ RACK 3 = **64**
T₁ I₁ S₁ S₁ U₁ E₁ S₁ RACK 4 = **57**
PAR SCORE 140-150   JUDD'S TOTAL **194**

50
E₁ M₃ B₃ A₁ R₁ G₂ O₁ RACK 1 = **65**
G₂ I₁ B₃ L₁ E₁ T₁ RACK 2 = **27**
A₁ L₁ L₁ E₁ R₁ G₂ Y₄ RACK 3 = **61**
H₄ E₁ R₁ P₃ E₁ S₁ RACK 4 = **11**
PAR SCORE 115-125   JUDD'S TOTAL **164**

51
M₃ I₁ S₁ T₁ I₁ M₃ E₁ RACK 1 = **61**
W₄ I₁ S₁ P₃ I₁ E₁ R₁ RACK 2 = **76**
S₁ N₁ I₁ V₄ E₁ L₁ RACK 3 = **13**
D₂ E₁ A₁ F₄ ☐ ☐ ☐ RACK 4 = **8**
PAR SCORE 95-105   JUDD'S TOTAL **158**

52
M₃ U₁ T₁ A₁ T₁ E₁ D₂ RACK 1 = **60**
C₃ A₁ N₁ I₁ N₁ E₁ RACK 2 = **16**
J₈ I₁ N₁ G₂ L₁ E₁ D₂ RACK 3 = **68**
H₄ U₁ N₁ G₂ E₁ R₁ RACK 4 = **10**
PAR SCORE 95-105   JUDD'S TOTAL **154**

53
R₁ U₁ F₄ F₄ I₁ A₁ N₁ RACK 1 = **63**
P₃ L₁ A₁ C₃ A₁ T₁ E₁ RACK 2 = **67**
I₁ N₁ V₄ A₁ D₂ E₁ RACK 3 = **30**
T₁ U₁ G₂ B₃ O₁ A₁ T₁ RACK 4 = **60**
PAR SCORE 140-150   JUDD'S TOTAL **220**

54
U₁ N₁ G₂ L₁ U₁ E₁ RACK 1 = **9**
V₄ I₁ C₃ T₁ O₁ R₁ RACK 2 = **33**
H₄ E₁ M₃ L₁ I₁ N₁ E₁ RACK 3 = **62**
B₃ O₁ D₂ I₁ L₁ Y₄ RACK 4 = **12**
PAR SCORE 70-80   JUDD'S TOTAL **116**

55
D₂ I₁ S₁ D₂ A₁ I₁ N₁ RACK 1 = **59**
M₃ U₁ L₁ L₁ E₁ T₁ RACK 2 = **16**
S₁ L₁ U₁ G₂ G₂ E₁ R₁ RACK 3 = **61**
P₃ E₁ R₁ F₄ U₁ M₃ E₁ RACK 4 = **64**
PAR SCORE 125-135   JUDD'S TOTAL **200**

56
S₁ T₁ O₁ I₁ C₃ ☐ ☐ RACK 1 = **7**
S₁ A₁ L₁ T₁ I₁ E₁ R₁ RACK 2 = **57**
T₁ W₄ I₁ T₁ C₃ H₄ Y₄ RACK 3 = **104**
D₂ O₁ M₃ A₁ I₁ N₁ RACK 4 = **9**
PAR SCORE 110-120   JUDD'S TOTAL **177**

57

H₄	E₁	A₁	R₁	T₁	Y₄		RACK 1 = **24**
S₁	T₁	A₁	R₁	L₁	E₁	T₁	RACK 2 = **57**
P₃	R₁	O₁	P₃	E₁	N₁	D₂	RACK 3 = **65**
B₃	Y₄	R₁	E₁				RACK 4 = **17**

PAR SCORE 100-110   JUDD'S TOTAL **163**

58

M₃	U₁	S₁	E₁	U₁	M₃		RACK 1 = **20**
B₃	I₁	S₁	C₃	U₁	I₁	T₁	RACK 2 = **61**
S₁	L₁	U₁	S₁	H₄	Y₄		RACK 3 = **12**
G₂	R₁	O₁	V₄	E₁	L₁		RACK 4 = **20**

PAR SCORE 70-80   JUDD'S TOTAL **113**

59

B₃	U₁	S₁	I₁	E₁	S₁	T₁	RACK 1 = **59**
H₄	A₁	W₄	K₅	E₁	R₁		RACK 2 = **24**
P₃	L₁	U₁	N₁	D₂	E₁	R₁	RACK 3 = **60**
T₁	R₁	O₁	U₁	P₃	E₁	R₁	RACK 4 = **77**

PAR SCORE 140-150   JUDD'S TOTAL **220**

60

B₃	E₁	H₄	I₁	N₁	D₂		RACK 1 = **16**
M₃	I₁	N₁	I₁	O₁	N₁		RACK 2 = **24**
B₃	E₁	M₃	U₁	S₁	E₁	D₂	RACK 3 = **62**
V₄	I₁	R₁	I₁	L₁	E₁		RACK 4 = **9**

PAR SCORE 70-80   JUDD'S TOTAL **111**

61

A₁	T₁	H₄	E₁	I₁	S₁	T₁	RACK 1 = **60**
O₁	R₁	A₁	C₃	L₁	E₁		RACK 2 = **16**
T₁	R₁	I₁	S₁	E₁	C₃	T₁	RACK 3 = **59**
A₁	X₈	E₁	D₂				RACK 4 = **36**

PAR SCORE 105-115   JUDD'S TOTAL **171**

62

V₄	I₁	O₁	L₁	E₁	N₁	T₁	RACK 1 = **60**
F₄	E₁	R₁	T₁	I₁	L₁	E₁	RACK 2 = **60**
C₃	R₁	U₁	I₁	S₁	E₁	R₁	RACK 3 = **60**
S₁	O₁	C₃	I₁	A₁	L₁		RACK 4 = **8**

PAR SCORE 120-130   JUDD'S TOTAL **188**

63

I₁	N₁	Q₁₀	U₁	I₁	R₁	Y₄	RACK 1 = **107**
R₁	I₁	P₃	T₁	I₁	D₂	E₁	RACK 2 = **60**
C₃	O₁	H₄	A₁	B₃	I₁	T₁	RACK 3 = **64**
B₃	L₁	I₁	M₃	P₃			RACK 4 = **14**

PAR SCORE 155-165   JUDD'S TOTAL **245**

64

S₁	H₄	E₁	L₁	V₄	E₁	S₁	RACK 1 = **64**
I₁	M₃	P₃	E₁	R₁	I₁	L₁	RACK 2 = **61**
F₄	I₁	N₁	E₁	R₁	Y₄		RACK 3 = **36**
U₁	N₁	I₁	O₁	N₁			RACK 4 = **5**

PAR SCORE 100-110   JUDD'S TOTAL **166**

65

F₄	I₁	S₁	H₄	Y₄			RACK 1 = **42**
W₄	E₁	E₁	P₃				RACK 2 = **9**
P₃	A₁	D₂	D₂	L₁	E₁	R₁	RACK 3 = **61**
T₁	I₁	G₂	R₁	E₁	S₁	S₁	RACK 4 = **60**

PAR SCORE 105-115   JUDD'S TOTAL **172**

66

A₁	R₁	T₁	F₄	U₁	L₁		RACK 1 = **17**
S₁	P₃	R₁	A₁	W₄	L₁		RACK 2 = **11**
I₁	N₁	S₁	T₁	E₁	A₁	D₂	RACK 3 = **58**
B₃	A₁	B₃	O₁	O₁	N₁		RACK 4 = **10**

PAR SCORE 55-65   JUDD'S TOTAL **96**

67

C₃	O₁	N₁	N₁	I₁	V₄	E₁		RACK 1 = **62**
P₃	O₁	S₁	T₁	A₁	L₁			RACK 2 = **16**
A₁	V₄	O₁	I₁	D₂	E₁	R₁		RACK 3 = **83**
C₃	A₁	S₁	C(blank)	A₁	D₂	E₁		RACK 4 = **59**

PAR SCORE 140-150 JUDD'S TOTAL **220**

68

V₄	A₁	G₂	A₁	R₁	Y₄			RACK 1 = **17**
O₁	X₈	I₁	D₂	I₁	Z₁₀	E₁		RACK 2 = **122**
F₄	O₁	R₁	G₂	O₁	T₁			RACK 3 = **10**
I₁	C₃	I₁	L₁	Y₄				RACK 4 = **10**

PAR SCORE 100-110 JUDD'S TOTAL **159**

69

S₁	T₁	A₁	R₁	C₃	H₄			RACK 1 = **11**
R₁	O₁	S₁	I₁	E₁	S₁	T₁		RACK 2 = **57**
C₃	O₁	G₂	E₁	N₁	T₁			RACK 3 = **27**
V₄	E₁	N₁	E₁	E₁	R₁			RACK 4 = **9**

PAR SCORE 70-80 JUDD'S TOTAL **104**

70

R₁	O₁	O₁	F₄	T₁	O₁	P₃		RACK 1 = **63**
H₄	A₁	Z₁₀	E₁	L₁				RACK 2 = **17**
W₄	A₁	S₁	P₃	Y₄				RACK 3 = **13**
T₁	R₁	I₁	C₃	O₁	T₁			RACK 4 = **24**

PAR SCORE 70-80 JUDD'S TOTAL **117**

71

C₃	L₁	I₁	Q₁₀	U₁	E₁	S₁		RACK 1 = **68**
G₂	U₁	L₁	C₃	H₄				RACK 2 = **22**
A₁	L₁	F₄	A₁	L(blank)	F₄	A₁		RACK 3 = **62**
T₁	R₁	U₁	A₁	N₁	T₁			RACK 4 = **6**

PAR SCORE 95-105 JUDD'S TOTAL **158**

72

D₂	I₁	A₁	M₃	O₁	N₁	D₂		RACK 1 = **83**
B₃	R₁	O₁	I₁	D₂	E₁	R₁		RACK 2 = **60**
T₁	O₁	D₂	D(blank)	Y₄				RACK 3 = **10**
L₁	A₁	I₁	T₁	Y₄				RACK 4 = **8**

PAR SCORE 100-110 JUDD'S TOTAL **161**

73

R₁	E₁	F₄	L₁	E₁	X₈			RACK 1 = **32**
M₃	A₁	N₁	S₁	I₁	O₁	N₁		RACK 2 = **59**
S₁	H₄	R₁	I₁	N₁	E₁			RACK 3 = **17**
C₃	A₁	V₄	I₁	T₁	Y₄			RACK 4 = **14**

PAR SCORE 75-85 JUDD'S TOTAL **122**

74

D₂	R₁	A₁	G₂	N₁	E₁	T₁		RACK 1 = **77**
M₃	O₁	O₁	N₁	L₁	I₁	T₁		RACK 2 = **59**
R₁	U₁	D₂	D₂	Y₄				RACK 3 = **10**
B₃	O₁	N₁	U₁	S₁				RACK 4 = **14**

PAR SCORE 100-110 JUDD'S TOTAL **160**

75

S₁	U₁	C₃	C(blank)	E₁	S₁	S₁		RACK 1 = **58**
M₃	O₁	N₁	K₅	E₁	Y₄			RACK 2 = **20**
J₈	A₁	Y₄						RACK 3 = **13**
F₄	U₁	S₁	I₁	O₁	N₁			RACK 4 = **17**

PAR SCORE 70-80 JUDD'S TOTAL **108**

76

K₅	N₁	O₁	T₁	T₁	Y₄			RACK 1 = **26**
L₁	E₁	M₃	O₁	N₁				RACK 2 = **13**
D₂	U₁	T₁	E₁	O₁	U₁	S₁		RACK 3 = **58**
T₁	E₁	N₁	S₁	I₁	O₁	N₁		RACK 4 = **57**

PAR SCORE 95-105 JUDD'S TOTAL **154**

77
RACK 1: P₃ R₁ O₁ T₁ E₁ G₂ E₁ = **60**
RACK 2: V₄ E₁ L₁ L₁ U₁ M₃ [blank] = **33**
RACK 3: I₁ N₁ E₁ X₈ A₁ C₃ T₁ = **66**
RACK 4: D₂ I₁ N₁ E₁ T₁ T₁ E₁ = **58**
PAR SCORE 135-145   JUDD'S TOTAL **217**

78
RACK 1: M₃ U₁ S₁ L₁ I₁ N₁ [blank] = **8**
RACK 2: P₃ L₁ U₁ N₁ G₂ E₁ R₁ = **61**
RACK 3: A₁ C₃ R₁ I₁ D₂ L₁ Y₄ = **63**
RACK 4: P₃ R₁ O₁ P[blank] H₄ E₁ T₁ = **72**
PAR SCORE 130-140   JUDD'S TOTAL **204**

79
RACK 1: T₁ R₁ U₁ I₁ S₁ M₃ [blank] = **24**
RACK 2: O₁ T₁ O₁ L₁ O₁ G₂ Y₄ = **61**
RACK 3: D₂ E₁ V₄ E₁ L₁ O₁ P₃ = **63**
RACK 4: B₃ R₁ A₁ I₁ Z₁₀ E₁ = **34**
PAR SCORE 115-125   JUDD'S TOTAL **182**

80
RACK 1: D₂ O₁ E₁ S₁ K₅ I₁ N₁ = **62**
RACK 2: F₄ U₁ R₁ L₁ = **14**
RACK 3: I₁ N₁ A₁ N₁ I₁ T₁ Y₄ = **60**
RACK 4: M₃ O₁ U₁ T₁ O₁ N₁ = **8**
PAR SCORE 90-100   JUDD'S TOTAL **144**

81
RACK 1: F₄ U₁ R₁ B₃ I₁ S₁ H₄ = **67**
RACK 2: N₁ U₁ P₃ T₁ I₁ A₁ L₁ = **59**
RACK 3: R₁ E₁ G₂ I₁ M₃ E₁ N₁ = **61**
RACK 4: B₃ A₁ R₁ O₁ N₁ Y₄ = **11**
PAR SCORE 125-135   JUDD'S TOTAL **198**

82
RACK 1: M₃ E₁ R₁ G₂ E₁ R₁ = **18**
RACK 2: O₁ U₁ T₁ W₄ A₁ I₁ T₁ = **60**
RACK 3: R₁ U₁ S₁ T₁ L₁ E₁ R₁ = **57**
RACK 4: T₁ Y₄ C₃ O₁ O₁ N₁ = **19**
PAR SCORE 95-105   JUDD'S TOTAL **154**

83
RACK 1: J₈ A₁ N₁ G₂ L₁ E₁ S₁ = **66**
RACK 2: H₄ A₁ N₁ D₂ F₄ U₁ L₁ = **64**
RACK 3: D₂ E₁ T₁ A₁ C₃ H₄ = **36**
RACK 4: P₃ I₁ R₁ A₁ T₁ E₁ = **8**
PAR SCORE 115-125   JUDD'S TOTAL **174**

84
RACK 1: A₁ N₁ I₁ M₃ I₁ S₁ M₃ = **63**
RACK 2: A₁ B₃ A₁ T₁ E₁ S₁ = **8**
RACK 3: L₁ Y₄ R₁ I₁ C₃ = **18**
RACK 4: C₃ O₁ R₁ O₁ N₁ E₁ R₁ = **59**
PAR SCORE 90-100   JUDD'S TOTAL **148**

85
RACK 1: L₁ I₁ N₁ G₂ U₁ A₁ L₁ = **58**
RACK 2: P₃ O₁ S₁ I₁ E₁ S₁ = **16**
RACK 3: T₁ R₁ I₁ N₁ A₁ R₁ Y₄ = **60**
RACK 4: G₂ R₁ O₁ U₁ P₃ E₁ R₁ = **64**
AR SCORE 135-145   JUDD'S TOTAL **198**

86
RACK 1: M₃ E₁ M₃ E₁ N₁ T₁ O₁ = **62**
RACK 2: F₄ O₁ H₄ = **9**
RACK 3: B₃ A₁ M[blank] B₃ O₁ O₁ = **15**
RACK 4: S₁ E₁ T₁ T₁ L₁ E₁ R₁ = **57**
PAR SCORE 85-95   JUDD'S TOTAL **143**

87

D₂ I₁ A₁ L₁ Y₄ Z₁₀ E₁ — RACK 1 = **72**
O₁ C₃ T₁ A₁ N₁ E₁ — RACK 2 = **8**
G₂ O₁ U₁ G₂ E₁ — RACK 3 = **7**
G₂ E₁ O₁ L₁ O₁ G(blank) Y₄ — RACK 4 = **60**

PAR SCORE 90-100   JUDD'S TOTAL **147**

88

C₃ O₁ M₃ R₁ A₁ D₂ E₁ — RACK 1 = **68**
P₃ E₁ N₁ T₁ A₁ N₁ E₁ — RACK 2 = **59**
E₁ C₃ L₁ A₁ I₁ R₁ — RACK 3 = **11**
K₅ I₁ L₁ L₁ J₈ O₁ Y₄ — RACK 4 = **113**

PAR SCORE 155-165   JUDD'S TOTAL **251**

89

D₂ U₁ A₁ L₁ I₁ T₁ Y₄ — RACK 1 = **61**
H₄ A₁ V₄ E₁ — RACK 2 = **30**
K₅ I₁ T₁ T₁ E₁ N₁ S₁ — RACK 3 = **61**
Q₁₀ U₁ E₁ E₁ N₁ L₁ Y₄ — RACK 4 = **69**

PAR SCORE 140-150   JUDD'S TOTAL **221**

90

A₁ N₁ O₁ D₂ A₁ L₁ — RACK 1 = **7**
C₃ R₁ I₁ M₃ S₁ O₁ N₁ — RACK 2 = **67**
F₄ A₁ R₁ A₁ W₄ A₁ Y₄ — RACK 3 = **67**
J₈ I₁ V₄ E₁ — RACK 4 = **14**

PAR SCORE 95-105   JUDD'S TOTAL **155**

91

V₄ I₁ B₃ R₁ A₁ T₁ O₁ — RACK 1 = **70**
T₁ E₁ N₁ F₄ O₁ L₁ D₂ — RACK 2 = **61**
Z₁₀ O₁ A₁ — RACK 3 = **24**
P₃ I₁ P₃ E₁ R₁ — RACK 4 = **9**

PAR SCORE 100-110   JUDD'S TOTAL **164**

92

C₃ A₁ M₃ P₃ H₄ O₁ R₁ — RACK 1 = **66**
E₁ M₃ B₃ E₁ D₂ — RACK 2 = **16**
R₁ H₄ Y₄ M(blank) E₁ R₁ S₁ — RACK 3 = **62**
O₁ L₁ D₂ E₁ N₁ — RACK 4 = **10**

PAR SCORE 95-105   JUDD'S TOTAL **154**

93

M₃ E₁ R₁ O₁ P₃ I₁ A₁ — RACK 1 = **62**
S₁ O₁ L₁ A₁ C₃ E₁ — RACK 2 = **8**
C₃ H₄ A₁ N₁ T₁ — RACK 3 = **30**
H₄ I₁ N₁ D₂ — RACK 4 = **16**

PAR SCORE 70-80   JUDD'S TOTAL **116**

94

F₄ A₁ I₁ L₁ U₁ R₁ E₁ — RACK 1 = **60**
H₄ O₁ L₁ I₁ S₁ M₃ — RACK 2 = **22**
C₃ O₁ N₁ J₈ O₁ I₁ N₁ — RACK 3 = **66**
B₃ L₁ O₁ N₁ D₂ — RACK 4 = **14**

PAR SCORE 100-110   JUDD'S TOTAL **162**

95

U₁ R₁ B₃ A₁ N₁ — RACK 1 = **10**
O₁ V₄ A₁ T₁ I₁ O₁ N₁ — RACK 2 = **60**
A₁ R₁ G₂ E₁ N₁ T₁ — RACK 3 = **11**
L₁ O₁ X₈ — RACK 4 = **26**

PAR SCORE 70-80   JUDD'S TOTAL **107**

96

G₂ L₁ O₁ W₄ E₁ R₁ — RACK 1 = **18**
V₄ I₁ T₁ I₁ A₁ T₁ E₁ — RACK 2 = **60**
S₁ M₃ I₁ T₁ H₄ Y₄ — RACK 3 = **14**
W₄ R₁ E₁ A₁ K₅ — RACK 4 = **12**

PAR SCORE 65-75   JUDD'S TOTAL **104**

97

E₁	X₈	T₁	R₁	E₁	M₃	E₁	RACK 1 =	**66**
C₃	H₄	R₁	O₁	M₃	A₁		RACK 2 =	**17**
B₃	E₁	N₁	I₁	G₂	N₁		RACK 3 =	**9**
S₁	A₁	L₁	T₁	I₁	N₁	E₁	RACK 4 =	**71**

PAR SCORE 100-110   JUDD'S TOTAL   **163**

98

T₁	W₄	E₁	L₁	F₄	T₁	H₄	RACK 1 =	**74**
V₄	E₁	S₁	P₃	E₁	R₁		RACK 2 =	**11**
M₃	O₁	R₁	A₁	S₁	S₁		RACK 3 =	**16**
W₄	O₁	M₃	A₁	N blank	L₁	Y₄	RACK 4 =	**64**

PAR SCORE 100-110   JUDD'S TOTAL   **165**

99

C₃	L₁	I₁	M₃	A₁	T₁	E₁	RACK 1 = **64**
B₃	E₁	C₃	K₅	O₁	N₁		RACK 2 = **42**
M₃	I₁	L₁	I₁	E₁	U₁		RACK 3 = **8**
A₁	P₃	H₄	I₁	D₂			RACK 4 = **19**

PAR SCORE 80-90   JUDD'S TOTAL   **133**

100

R₁	O₁	M₃	A₁	I₁	N₁	E₁	RACK 1 = **61**
S₁	T₁	E₁	T₁	S₁	O₁	N₁	RACK 2 = **57**
R₁	E₁	C₃	O₁	U₁	P₃		RACK 3 = **13**
F₄	E₁	S₁	T₁	E₁	R₁		RACK 4 = **9**

PAR SCORE 85-95   JUDD'S TOTAL   **140**

101

T₁	O₁	R₁	R₁	I₁	D₂		RACK 1 = **14**
W₄	H₄	I₁	N₁	E₁	S₁		RACK 2 = **12**
M₃	U₁	T₁	A₁	B₃	L₁	E₁	RACK 3 = **83**
S₁	O₁	I₁	L₁	A₁	G₂	E₁	RACK 4 = **58**

PAR SCORE 105-115   JUDD'S TOTAL   **167**

102

V₄	E₁	N₁	O₁	U₁	S₁		RACK 1 = **9**
L₁	E blank	A₁	R₁	N₁	E₁	D₂	RACK 2 = **59**
I₁	C₃	E₁	C₃	A₁	P₃		RACK 3 = **24**
B₃	E₁	R₁	A₁	T₁	E₁	D₂	RACK 4 = **60**

PAR SCORE 95-105   JUDD'S TOTAL   **152**

103

A₁	P₃	O₁	L₁	O₁	G₂	Y₄	RACK 1 = **63**
F₄	O₁	O₁	L₁	I₁	S₁	H₄	RACK 2 = **89**
J₈	I₁	B₃	E₁	R₁	S₁		RACK 3 = **23**
S₁	K₅	E₁	T₁	C₃	H₄		RACK 4 = **15**

PAR SCORE 120-130   JUDD'S TOTAL   **190**

104

V₄	A₁	C₃	U₁	U₁	M₃		RACK 1 = **39**
S₁	N₁	E₁	E₁	Z₁₀	E₁	S₁	RACK 2 = **66**
M₃	A₁	R₁	S₁	H₄			RACK 3 = **30**
G₂	E₁	N₁	I₁	U₁	S₁		RACK 4 = **7**

PAR SCORE 85-95   JUDD'S TOTAL   **142**

105

C₃	A₁	M₃	B₃	R₁	I₁	C₃	RACK 1 = **65**
V₄	O₁	C blank	A₁	L₁	L₁	Y₄	RACK 2 = **74**
I₁	N₁	N₁	A₁	T₁	E₁		RACK 3 = **6**
E₁	Q₁₀	U₁	I₁	T₁	Y₄		RACK 4 = **54**

PAR SCORE 125-135   JUDD'S TOTAL   **199**

106

T₁	H₄	I₁	C₃	K₅	E₁	T₁	RACK 1 = **73**
S₁	M₃	I₁	R₁	C₃	H₄		RACK 2 = **13**
Z₁₀	A₁	P₃					RACK 3 = **28**
P₃	Y₄	L₁	O₁	N₁			RACK 4 = **18**

PAR SCORE 80-90   JUDD'S TOTAL   **132**

107

G$_2$	U$_1$	N$_1$	P$_3$	L$_1$	A$_1$	Y$_4$	RACK 1 = **63**
B$_3$	L$_1$	O$_1$	U$_1$	S$_1$	E$_1$		RACK 2 = **24**
A$_1$	R$_1$	O$_1$	U$_1$	S$_1$	A$_1$	L$_1$	RACK 3 = **57**
G$_2$	A$_1$	R$_1$	M$_3$	E$_1$	N$_1$	T$_1$	RACK 4 = **60**

PAR SCORE 125-135   JUDD'S TOTAL **204**

108

W$_4$	O$_1$	O$_1$	L$_{blank}$	I$_1$	E$_1$	R$_1$	RACK 1 = **60**
C$_3$	L$_1$	E$_1$	R$_1$	I$_1$	S$_1$	Y$_4$	RACK 2 = **62**
B$_3$	L$_1$	A$_1$	T$_1$	A$_1$	N$_1$	T$_1$	RACK 3 = **68**
T$_1$	R$_1$	E$_1$	S$_1$	T$_1$	L$_1$	E$_1$	RACK 4 = **57**

PAR SCORE 165-175   JUDD'S TOTAL **247**

109

M$_3$	O$_1$	L$_1$	L$_1$	I$_1$	F$_4$	Y$_4$	RACK 1 = **67**
G$_2$	A$_1$	Z$_{10}$	E$_1$	L$_1$	L$_1$	E$_1$	RACK 2 = **77**
T$_1$	R$_1$	I$_1$	V$_4$	I$_1$	A$_1$		RACK 3 = **9**
R$_1$	A$_1$	Y$_4$	O$_1$	N$_1$			RACK 4 = **16**

PAR SCORE 105-115   JUDD'S TOTAL **169**

110

P$_3$	A$_1$	R$_1$	T$_1$	I$_1$	E$_1$	D$_2$	RACK 1 = **60**
L$_1$	Y$_4$	C$_3$	E$_1$	U$_1$	M$_3$		RACK 2 = **21**
T$_1$	A$_1$	I$_1$	L$_1$	O$_1$	R$_1$	S$_1$	RACK 3 = **57**
C$_3$	O$_1$	N$_1$	C$_{blank}$	U$_1$	R$_1$	S$_1$	RACK 4 = **58**

PAR SCORE 135-145   JUDD'S TOTAL **196**

111

A$_1$	N$_1$	N$_1$	O$_1$	Y$_4$			RACK 1 = **16**
N$_1$	U$_1$	D$_2$	I$_1$	S$_1$	M$_3$		RACK 2 = **9**
L$_1$	A$_1$	T$_1$	T$_1$	I$_1$	C$_3$	E$_1$	RACK 3 = **61**
H$_4$	U$_1$	N$_1$	K$_5$	E$_1$	R$_1$	S$_1$	RACK 4 = **64**

PAR SCORE 95-105   JUDD'S TOTAL **150**

112

U$_1$	X$_8$	O$_1$	R$_1$	I$_1$	A$_1$	L$_1$	RACK 1 = **80**
P$_3$	O$_1$	R$_1$	K$_5$	E$_1$	R$_1$		RACK 2 = **12**
W$_4$	O$_1$	M$_3$	A$_1$	N$_1$	L$_1$	Y$_4$	RACK 3 = **95**
G$_2$	H$_4$	O$_1$	U$_1$	L$_1$			RACK 4 = **17**

PAR SCORE 125-135   JUDD'S TOTAL **204**

113

C$_3$	L$_1$	I$_1$	M$_3$	B$_3$			RACK 1 = **33**
J$_8$	E$_1$	R$_1$	S$_1$	E$_1$	Y$_4$		RACK 2 = **16**
D$_2$	E$_1$	F$_4$	L$_1$	A$_1$	T$_1$	E$_1$	RACK 3 = **65**
N$_1$	A$_1$	P$_3$	H$_4$	T$_1$	H$_4$	A$_1$	RACK 4 = **65**

PAR SCORE 110-120   JUDD'S TOTAL **179**

114

S$_1$	U$_1$	B$_3$	O$_1$	R$_1$	N$_1$		RACK 1 = **8**
W$_4$	A$_1$	S$_1$	H$_4$	E$_1$	R$_1$		RACK 2 = **16**
T$_1$	R$_1$	O$_1$	U$_1$	G$_2$	H$_4$		RACK 3 = **20**
C$_3$	U$_1$	M$_3$	Q$_{10}$	U$_{blank}$	A$_1$	T$_1$	RACK 4 = **71**

PAR SCORE 70-80   JUDD'S TOTAL **115**

115

B$_3$	E$_1$	S$_1$	M$_3$	U$_1$	T$_1$		RACK 1 = **16**
R$_1$	A$_1$	G$_2$	T$_1$	A$_1$	G$_2$		RACK 2 = **8**
A$_1$	P$_3$	P$_3$	A$_1$	L$_1$	L$_1$		RACK 3 = **20**
M$_3$	O$_1$	U$_1$	R$_1$	N$_1$	E$_1$	R$_1$	RACK 4 = **59**

PAR SCORE 65-75   JUDD'S TOTAL **103**

116

H$_4$	A$_1$	I$_1$	R$_1$	P$_3$	I$_1$	N$_1$	RACK 1 = **86**
I$_1$	N$_1$	T$_1$	O$_1$	N$_1$	E$_1$		RACK 2 = **6**
O$_1$	P$_3$	E$_1$	R$_1$	A$_1$	N$_1$	T$_1$	RACK 3 = **59**
E$_1$	L$_1$	E$_1$	C$_3$	T$_1$	R$_1$	O$_1$	RACK 4 = **65**

PAR SCORE 145-155   JUDD'S TOTAL **216**

117

P₃ A₁ R₁ S₁ L₁ E₁ Y₄ RACK 1 = 63
G₂ E₁ C₃ K₅ O₁ RACK 2 = 36
C₃ H₄ A₁ N₁ C(blank) E₁ L₁ RACK 3 = 61
A₁ L₁ C₃ H₄ E₁ M₃ Y₄ RACK 4 = 78
PAR SCORE 150-160   JUDD'S TOTAL 238

118

R₁ E₁ V₄ E₁ N₁ G₂ E₁ RACK 1 = 62
I₁ N₁ B₃ U₁ I₁ L₁ T₁ RACK 2 = 59
P₃ O₁ N₁ T₁ O₁ O₁ N₁ RACK 3 = 59
V₄ I₁ O₁ L₁ A₁ RACK 4 = 16
PAR SCORE 125-135   JUDD'S TOTAL 196

119

T₁ R₁ O₁ O₁ P₃ E₁ R₁ RACK 1 = 59
S₁ C₃ A₁ N₁ T₁ L₁ Y₄ RACK 2 = 64
O₁ D₂ I₁ O₁ U₁ S₁ RACK 3 = 7
L₁ U₁ R₁ K₅ RACK 4 = 24
PAR SCORE 95-105   JUDD'S TOTAL 154

120

F₄ O₁ G₂ H₄ O₁ R₁ N₁ RACK 1 = 80
L₁ A₁ C₃ T₁ A₁ R₁ Y₄ RACK 2 = 62
N₁ O₁ U₁ G₂ A₁ T₁ RACK 3 = 14
W₄ A₁ N₁ T₁ O₁ N₁ RACK 4 = 9
PAR SCORE 100-110   JUDD'S TOTAL 165

121

V₄ O₁ D₂ K₅ A₁ RACK 1 = 39
T₁ I₁ G₂ H₄ T₁ E₁ N₁ RACK 2 = 61
P₃ A₁ T₁ T₁ E₁ R₁ N₁ RACK 3 = 59
B₃ U₁ Y₄ S₁ RACK 4 = 18
PAR SCORE 110-120   JUDD'S TOTAL 177

122

H₄ O₁ P₃ S₁ A₁ C₃ K₅ RACK 1 = 70
E₁ X₈ T₁ A₁ N₁ T₁ RACK 2 = 13
A₁ N₁ A₁ T₁ O₁ M₃ Y₄ RACK 3 = 74
C₃ O₁ R₁ I₁ U₁ M₃ RACK 4 = 10
PAR SCORE 105-115   JUDD'S TOTAL 167

123

S₁ C₃ I₁ S₁ S₁ O₁ R₁ RACK 1 = 61
L₁ O₁ B₃ A₁ T₁ E₁ RACK 2 = 11
E₁ Y₄ E₁ S₁ H₄ O₁ T₁ RACK 3 = 63
L₁ A₁ N₁ K₅ Y₄ RACK 4 = 24
PAR SCORE 95-105   JUDD'S TOTAL 159

124

A₁ L₁ W₄ A₁ Y₄ S₁ RACK 1 = 20
C₃ H₄ A₁ M₃ O₁ I₁ S₁ RACK 2 = 64
F₄ L₁ A₁ M₃ E₁ RACK 3 = 30
M(blank) I₁ S₁ R₁ U₁ L₁ E₁ RACK 4 = 56
PAR SCORE 105-115   JUDD'S TOTAL 170

125

G₂ A₁ I₁ E₁ T₁ Y₄ RACK 1 = 10
L₁ O₁ G₂ I₁ C₃ A₁ L₁ RACK 2 = 70
P₃ R₁ E₁ L₁ A₁ T₁ E₁ RACK 3 = 59
S₁ A₁ U₁ C₃ Y₄ RACK 4 = 10
PAR SCORE 90-100   JUDD'S TOTAL 149

126

U₁ N₁ I₁ Q₁₀ U₁ E₁ RACK 1 = 35
M₃ I₁ G₂ R₁ A₁ N₁ T₁ RACK 2 = 60
D₂ E₁ F₄ I₁ L₁ E₁ RACK 3 = 20
D₂ E₁ A₁ C₃ O₁ N₁ RACK 4 = 9
PAR SCORE 75-85   JUDD'S TOTAL 124

127 B_{blank} O_1 B_3 B_3 I_1 N_1 S_1 RACK 1 = **66**
A_1 M_3 M_3 I_1 N_1 O_1 RACK 2 = **10**
F_4 O_1 R_1 E_1 G_2 O_1 RACK 3 = **10**
O_1 C_3 E_1 A_1 N_1 RACK 4 = **21**
PAR SCORE 65-75 JUDD'S TOTAL **107**

128 R_1 I_1 M_3 L_1 E_1 S_1 S_1 RACK 1 = **65**
T_1 E_1 X_8 T_1 U_1 A_1 L_1 RACK 2 = **92**
V_4 O_1 Y_4 E_1 U_1 R_1 S_1 RACK 3 = **63**
Z_{10} O_1 U_1 N_1 D_2 S_1 RACK 4 = **48**
PAR SCORE 170-180 JUDD'S TOTAL **268**

129 L_1 I_1 A_1 B_3 L_1 E_1 RACK 1 = **14**
P_3 I_1 A_1 N_1 O_1 S_1 RACK 2 = **8**
S_1 O_1 P_3 I_1 T_1 E_1 RACK 3 = **8**
T_1 E_1 N_1 U_1 I_1 T_1 Y_4 RACK 4 = **80**
PAR SCORE 65-75 JUDD'S TOTAL **110**

130 P_3 E_1 R_1 I_1 O_1 D_2 RACK 1 = **18**
D_2 E_1 I_1 F_4 O_1 R_1 M_3 RACK 2 = **63**
M_3 E_1 N_1 T_1 A_1 L_1 RACK 3 = **11**
A_1 I_1 R_1 W_4 A_1 V_4 E_1 RACK 4 = **63**
PAR SCORE 95-105 JUDD'S TOTAL **155**

131 F_4 O_1 X_8 F_4 I_1 R_1 E_1 RACK 1 = **86**
G_2 I_1 R_1 T_1 E_1 D_2 RACK 2 = **8**
S_1 T_1 O_1 O_1 G_2 E_1 RACK 3 = **7**
J_8 A_1 U_1 N_1 T_1 Y_4 RACK 4 = **48**
PAR SCORE 90-100 JUDD'S TOTAL **149**

132 V_4 E_1 S_1 T_1 A_1 L_1 RACK 1 = **9**
W_4 R_1 O_1 U_1 G_2 H_4 T_1 RACK 2 = **78**
L_1 Y_4 S_1 I_1 N_1 E_1 RACK 3 = **9**
Q_{10} U_1 A_1 L_1 I_1 T_1 Y_4 RACK 4 = **107**
PAR SCORE 125-135 JUDD'S TOTAL **203**

133 E_1 L_1 E_1 C_3 T_1 O_1 R_1 RACK 1 = **59**
B_3 R_1 A_1 V_4 A_1 D_2 O_1 RACK 2 = **71**
B_3 A_1 C_3 K_5 U_1 P_3 RACK 3 = **48**
P_3 E_1 T_1 T_1 I_1 L_1 Y_4 RACK 4 = **62**
PAR SCORE 150-160 JUDD'S TOTAL **240**

134 H_4 A_1 T_1 B_3 A_1 N_1 D_2 RACK 1 = **63**
F_4 R_1 E_1 A_1 K_5 Y_4 RACK 2 = **48**
P_3 A_1 L_1 A_1 C_3 E_1 RACK 3 = **20**
S_1 L_1 U_1 R_1 P_3 RACK 4 = **7**
PAR SCORE 85-95 JUDD'S TOTAL **138**

135 P_3 R_1 E_1 W_4 A_1 S_1 H_4 RACK 1 = **73**
I_1 T_1 E_1 R_1 A_1 T_1 E_1 RACK 2 = **57**
C_3 A_1 N_1 Z_{10} O_1 N_1 E_1 RACK 3 = **88**
A_1 S_1 T_1 O_1 N_1 Y_4 RACK 4 = **9**
PAR SCORE 145-155 JUDD'S TOTAL **227**

136 C_3 O_1 R_1 R_1 E_1 C_3 T_1 RACK 1 = **61**
G_2 L_1 E_1 E_1 F_4 U_1 L_1 RACK 2 = **61**
M_3 O_1 R_1 T_1 A_1 R_1 Y_4 RACK 3 = **74**
U_1 L_1 T_1 I_1 M_3 O_1 RACK 4 = **16**
PAR SCORE 135-145 JUDD'S TOTAL **212**

137

F_4	O_1	U_1	N_1	D_2	R_1	Y_4	RACK 1 =	**64**
G_2	U_1	R_1	G_2	L_1	E_1	D_2	RACK 2	**62**
O_1	P_3	A_1	L_1	I_1	N_1	E_1	RACK 3	**62**
R_1	E_1	A_1	L_1	I_1	Z_{10}	E_1	RACK 4	**98**

PAR SCORE 180-190   JUDD'S TOTAL **286**

138

S_1	I_1	L_1	I_1	C_3	A_1		RACK 1 =	**16**
W_4	A_1	X_8	I_1	E_1	S_1	T_1	RACK 2	**67**
R_1	A_1	M_3	P_3	A_1	R_1	T_1	RACK 3	**61**
N_1	A_1	T_1	I_1	O_1	N_1		RACK 4	**6**

PAR SCORE 95-105   JUDD'S TOTAL **150**

139

F_4	I_1	S_1	S_1	I_1	O_1	N_1	RACK 1 =	**60**
A_1	R_1	M_3	P_3	I_1	T_1		RACK 2	**16**
C_3	A_1	S_1	I_1	N_1	O_1		RACK 3	**16**
L_1	U_1	R_1	C_3	H_4			RACK 4	**10**

PAR SCORE 60-70   JUDD'S TOTAL **102**

140

C_3	I_1	L_1	I_1	U_1	M_3		RACK 1 =	**16**
G_2	L_1	A_1	S_1	S_1	Y_4		RACK 2	**10**
R_1	E_1	F_4	R_1	E_1	S_1	H_4	RACK 3	**67**
S_1	T_1	E_1	W_4	A_1	R_1	D_2	RACK 4	**61**

PAR SCORE 95-105   JUDD'S TOTAL **154**

141

C_3	O_1	L_1	L_1	U_1	D_2	E_1	RACK 1 =	**60**
A_1	M_3	O_1	R_1	I_1	S_1	T_1	RACK 2	**65**
C_3	O_1	O_1	K_5	E_1	R_1	Y_4	RACK 3	**98**
P_3	R_1	O_1	F_4	A_1	N_1	E_1	RACK 4	**62**

PAR SCORE 180-190   JUDD'S TOTAL **285**

142

T_1	H_4	U_1	M_3	B_3			RACK 1 =	**24**
C_3	U_1	N_1	E_1	A_1	T_1	E_1	RACK 2 =	**59**
I_1	N_1	N_1	A_1	R_1	D_2	S_1	RACK 3	**58**
O_1	X_8	L_1	I_1	P_3			RACK 4 =	**42**

PAR SCORE 115-125   JUDD'S TOTAL **183**

143

S_1	C_3	U_1	L_1	P_3	I_1	N_1	RACK 1 =	**64**
U_1	G_2	L_1	I_1	E_1	S_1	T_1	RACK 2 =	**58**
V_4	A_1	G_2	I_1	L_1	E_1		RACK 3 =	**30**
E_1	M_3	B_3	L_1	E_1	M_3		RACK 4 -	**12**

PAR SCORE 100-110   JUDD'S TOTAL **164**

144

K_5	N_1	E_1	E_1	L_1	E_1	R_1	RACK 1 =	**61**
O_1	R_1	E_1	G_2	A_1	N_1	O_1	RACK 2 -	**62**
S_1	A_1	U_1	C_3	E_1			RACK 3 -	**14**
T_1	R_1	A_1	I_1	N_1	E_1	E_1	RACK 4 -	**57**

PAR SCORE 120-130   JUDD'S TOTAL **194**

145

W_4	A_1	G_2	T_1	A_1	I_1	L_1	RACK 1 =	**61**
Z_{10}	E_1	U_1	G_2	M_3	A_1		RACK 2 =	**54**
S_1	P_3	I_1	R_1	A_1	N_1	T_1	RACK 3 =	**59**
H_4	O_1	M_3	I_1	L_1	Y_4		RACK 4 =	**14**

PAR SCORE 115-125   JUDD'S TOTAL **188**

146

F_4	L_1	A_1	G_2	O_1	N_1		RACK 1 =	**20**
A_1	U_1	C_3	T_1	I_1	O_1	N_1	RACK 2 =	**65**
A_1	M_3	N_1	E_1	S_1	I_1	C_3	RACK 3 =	**61**
L_1	E_1	N_1	D_2	E_1	R_1		RACK 4 =	**7**

PAR SCORE 95-105   JUDD'S TOTAL **153**

147

P₃ E₁ P₃ S₁ I₁ N₁ ☐ RACK 1 = **20**

O₁ L₁ D₂ I₁ S₁ H₄ ☐ RACK 2 = **10**

H₄ O₁ R₁ I₁ Z₁₀ O₁ N₁ RACK 3 = **107**

C₃ A₁ N₁ T₁ L₁ E₁ S₁ RACK 4 = **59**

PAR SCORE 120-130   JUDD'S TOTAL   **196**

148

D₂ A₁ N₁ D₂ I₁ L₁ Y₄ RACK 1 = **62**

G₂ I₁ N₁ G₂ H₄ A₁ M₃ RACK 2 = **64**

P₃ U₁ R₁ S₁ U₁ E₁ R₁ RACK 3 = **60**

N₁ A₁ V₄ E₁ L₁ ☐ ☐ RACK 4 = **16**

PAR SCORE 125-135   JUDD'S TOTAL   **202**

149

E₁ N₁ W₄ I₁ N₁ D₂ ☐ RACK 1 = **18**

F₄ O₁ R₁ E₁ R₁ U₁ N₁ RACK 2 = **60**

M₃ A₁ X₈ I₁ L₁ L₁ A₁ RACK 3 = **82**

O₁ V₄ E₁ R₁ T₁ ☐ ☐ RACK 4 = **12**

PAR SCORE 105-115   JUDD'S TOTAL   **172**

150

P₃ H₄ A₁ S₁ M₃ I₁ D₂ RACK 1 = **73**

S₁ C₃ O₁ L₁ L₁ O₁ P₃ RACK 2 = **61**

W₄ E₁ N₁ C₃ H₄ ☐ ☐ RACK 3 = **16**

Y₄ O₁ U₁ N₁ G₂ ☐ ☐ RACK 4 = **9**

PAR SCORE 95-105   JUDD'S TOTAL   **159**